# IT CAN HAPPEN
# TO YOU

# IT Can Happen TO YOU

*by Ernest Holmes
and Willis Kinnear*

SCIENCE OF MIND MAGAZINE
Los Angeles, California

*Published by* SCIENCE OF MIND MAGAZINE
3251 West Sixth Street, Los Angeles 5, California

Copyright © 1959 by Ernest Holmes and Willis Kinnear
Printed in the United States of America

## CONTENTS

|  |  | Page |
|---|---|---|
| *Introduction* | | 7 |
| I | You Are the Judge | 9 |
| II | There's a Reason for Everything | 17 |
| III | The Price of Health | 25 |
| IV | Your Crisis for Today | 38 |
| V | Ask, and You Receive | 48 |
| VI | Are You a Statistic? | 58 |
| VII | Calamities Can Be Opportunities | 67 |
| VIII | You Have Limitless Resources | 77 |
| IX | The Way Things Happen | 85 |
| X | It *Can* Happen to You! | 90 |
| *Acknowledgments* | | 96 |

# INTRODUCTION

It can happen to you!

You ask, "What can happen to me?"

Well, what do you want to happen?

Not only you but every one of your friends has a long, long list of things he desires to experience. Some of these things seem very likely to happen, others are just remote possibilities; then there is that large group of "things desired" which appears to be completely in the realm of wishful thinking, entirely impossible.

But what is it that causes what you want to happen actually to become a tangible experience? Is there some process to be learned? some secret to be sought out? some hocus-pocus to be indulged in?

Actually nothing of this kind is involved.

Suppose you are standing in the middle of a room. You are tired of standing. You want to be seated comfortably in a chair. What do you do? You decide to be seated in a comfortable chair. You make up your mind that this is going to "happen," and you proceed to move to the chair of your choice and place yourself in it. There is no argument in your mind about what you want to occur, no hesitancy in picking out the chair you want to sit in, no doubting whether you are able to get there or that the chair will be there when you arrive.

Simple? Very much so.

But the amazing thing about this illustration is the fact that the same sort of thing is happening to you every moment of your life. All day long many different kinds of things happen to you, and they are all results of mental decisions relating to your experience and concern your health, affairs, or relationships.

*It can happen to you!*

What?

What you think about, combined with the way you feel and act concerning what you think! Nothing in your life is exempt from these influencing factors.

This book shows you the way you can experience the things you desire. In one sense of the word it is a "do it yourself" project, for irrespective of what kind of experience it is you desire, you are responsible for the "doing." The proof that it can be done is contained in the many true stories, case histories, of those who have "done it," who have had what they desire become part of their experience.

NOTE: *Identification of the reference numbers which appear through the book may be found on page 96.*

## CHAPTER I

## YOU ARE THE JUDGE

You are in the unique position of being both the judge and the jury in your life and experience. You weigh all the evidence in connection with any situation or problem and after due deliberation announce your verdict. The sentence or penalty involved is one that you cannot avoid.

Sometimes it is not even necessary for you to come to a verdict of your own, instead you may readily accept ones that others have pronounced for you.

This immediately raises the questions: What are you doing to yourself? How valid are the verdicts you have reached or accepted? What kind of a sentence are you serving or what kind of a penalty are you paying? How much are you depriving yourself of health, abundance, love, joy, happiness, and the other things that make life worth living?

There is probably not a person living who has not in some respect limited his experience of the good life has to offer. But regardless of the manner in which you may find yourself limited there are always ways and means for you to cast off such shackles and discover a new freedom.

Every waking moment you are arriving at a verdict concerning yourself; you are making a decision, you are choosing, deciding what kind of a life you will have.

You can learn to be a better judge. You can discover a way to keep from stacking the jury against yourself. You can find a way to better evaluate the evidence. And of utmost importance, you can learn always to arrive at a verdict that is in your favor, a verdict of freedom instead of bondage.

There are those who have realized that much of the evidence offered to justify a verdict imposing limitation was not necessarily valid, and refused to further accept the verdict and released themselves from its bondage.

This is what you want to happen to you. It can happen to you. You can enjoy a fuller, richer life.

Just how does this work in practical everyday living?

Let us consider the case of Miranda S. Walton.[1]

*The Evidence:* Crippling arthritis.

*The Verdict:* Pain and suffering, and a limited experience of living.

*The story of the cripple who walked again:*

> Three years ago I had resigned myself to being partially, if not completely, incapacitated by arthritis. Everywhere, including the medical world, I heard the same verdict: There is no cure for arthritis. The advice given me was to keep as well as possible in other ways, and to learn to adjust to such a life. I will have to admit I felt rather smug when my doctor, my friends, and my family complimented me on how nicely I was adjusting to being a cripple. It is true that I had many interests which seemed to fill my life; and with modern painkillers I felt that, if I had to accept such a life, I would do it gracefully.
>
> But the time came when a wheel chair no longer sufficed; I became bedfast. But I was still determined to "make the best of it"! I felt as long as I had my beloved books, my radio for the wakeful nights of pain, and friends to visit me, I had many blessings. And I do not deny that all these things helped me through a very bad time.
>
> As the weeks and months passed, it became harder to resign myself to such a future. Then a wonderful thing happened; it began with a magazine. I am a person who reads just about everything, so when a friend of my daughter's sent me a copy of *Science of Mind* Magazine I naturally devoured its contents.

There was an article in it on faith. I did not know then how great a part it would play in my life, so I passed the copy along to another friend, and now I fail to remember the issue or the writer. But whoever it was, he or she started me on the way back to health. The thought which was deeply planted in my mind was this: Faith must be *active*. The article proceeded to enlarge on how so many people will pray for health and other blessings, then sit still and expect God to touch them and heal them. The accusation hit home. Those words were meant for me. I had prayed, and friends had prayed for my recovery, but all the time I had been lying still, doing nothing about it. I now began to read all I could get along this line, including *This Thing Called Life* by Dr. Ernest Holmes. And I began to practice what I read.

Then one day I felt I was ready. I was alone that afternoon and I began pulling myself up to a sitting position. Of course it was hard. When one's mind is conditioned to pain and hopelessness for years, it takes time to undo the damage of the decades of wrong thinking. But I did it. The next day I achieved sitting on the side of the bed, and the day after that I bore the weight of my feet on the floor. I continued studying and putting into practice the things I learned. In a month I was able to walk across the room, but also made use of a wheel chair. Then I realized what a crutch my chair had become, and I had it taken from the house. Instead of viewing myself on the morrow as sitting in a chair sewing, I visualized myself as *walking,* doing the many things I enjoyed. At night, instead of using pacifiers to fill the pain-filled hours, I imagined myself walking along the seashore or in the pine woods I loved so well. And, above all, I refused pity and help from family and friends. I think that was the hardest thing to overcome. So many times when I would begin to walk or do some work they would say, "Be careful, you have arthritis, you should not do that." It took real mental gymnastics to overcome their loving solicitude.

But the result? It was January, 1957, when I took my first big step toward health. Today I am doing my own work; I have no pain from arthritis. And I am happy with that inward joy which Don Blanding spoke of in his immortal poetry. I have learned that only I can render a verdict concerning myself. I am the master of my soul. And I refuse to be a cripple.

\* \* \*

What is there of value in this true story that might be of help to you? No, you don't have to have arthritis to benefit from the lesson it contains.

First, there was the fact that this woman did have arthritis. Second, she accepted the verdict that nothing could be done about it. Third, she was serving the sentence she had accepted for herself.

Then there came a time when she discovered that perhaps the evidence had been misinterpreted. This did not mean that she did not have arthritis, but rather that behind the evidence, the appearance, there was something else which caused it to appear.

The conviction she had in the necessity of her undesirable condition was transferred to a conviction, an active creative faith, in the ability of Life to express Itself in and through her in a normal and natural manner free of crippling limitations.

This was the new verdict she declared for herself, which freed her from previous ones relating to her condition. She had determined to have the right things, the good things she desired, start happening to her.

Sometimes a new verdict may be rendered with immediate and startling results.

Most men have a strong sense of responsibility toward their wives and children. The husband is the guy who has to provide the "wherewithal" to keep the family supplied with all its needs.

A sort of panic creeps in whenever the "wherewithal" is threatened in any way. This is felt by both husband and wife.

The case of Christopher West[2] provides a dramatic and remarkable illustration of how the slate may literally be wiped clean and a completely new start made.

*The Evidence:* A man hopelessly down and out.
*The Verdict:* No favorable solution.
*The story of a new-found experience of living:*

> Five years ago, although I had the best of intentions, I made a hash of my life. With dozens of books in my own library on prayer, meditation, contemplation, positive thinking, and many others, I let my experiences get out of control. I had read all the books with a purely *intellectual* interest. I had studied them as interesting phenomena. I profited nothing.
>
> Through a seeming whirlwind of circumstances my whole life, as well as my new family's life, was in a shambles: my wife was in critical condition in a hospital; our newborn daughter was just barely breathing; and I was faced with a complex legal suit. My job was with a firm whose precarious finances made each pay check a big question mark. I had worried and blustered and begged.
>
> One night I found myself without even twenty-five cents to buy a gallon of gasoline to get to the hospital for visiting hours. Desperation was too mild a word for my mental condition. I sank to my knees in our apartment, and gave up! There was nothing further I could do, and I said so aloud. I had exhausted myself running around in circles. But now, suddenly, I shut off my own muddled day-to-day thinking.
>
> There was no answering "blinding light." God did not "speak" to me. But I went to bed and I slept. In full and complete faith that Someone or Something had

been contacted and that my problems were being solved, I slept as I hadn't slept for months.

Hours later the apartment doorbell rang. I awoke and stumbled through the darkness to the door. A woman, whom my wife and I had known only casually, stood there. She reached out and pressed an envelope into my hand saying, "This is for your wife and baby."

I mumbled my thanks for what I thought was a pretty card, bade her good night, closed the door, threw the envelope on the table, went back to bed and slept until dawn.

That morning I hadn't a trace of worry. I whistled and hummed through my shower and shave. Then I remembered the envelope and opened it. In it was fifty dollars! That is not a great sum of money. But to a man who didn't even have enough money to get to work, fifty dollars was a fortune. This answer to prayer was the turning point.

Once I had my cluttered and confused thinking out of the way, people *literally* "came from all directions" to help. An unknown garageman repaired our car free of charge; a breadman rounded up other drivers to give blood transfusions to my wife; the hospital waived most of the many, many hospital charges. I soon brought my wife and daughter home from the hospital in good health, and even more people arrived to volunteer help. The lawsuit against me was dropped!

All this because I finally turned to man's unfailing Source of supply — God!

This is the secret of scientific prayer as I found it to be: The mightiest Force in the universe does through us what we let It do. We are channels for Divine action when we get our concepts of limitation out of the way. But we must first consciously contact the Divine Presence. And that is where prayer or affirmation comes in. They help us to accept the creative Power for Good known as God.

Since that eventful night, I have realized that my thinking was too often like a mouse scurrying in a maze. When business and financial problems press in, I have learned to use a simplified method in the practice of the Presence of God. Four simple words: *God is with me*. To me, these sum up the essence of all the teachings I have ever read.

I can't plead lack of time to make this simple utterance. I can face any problem, any circumstance, with this affirmation. When I do, there emerges an increased spiritual awareness. Then, as Ernest Holmes has repeatedly said, "Divine Intelligence takes hold of our consciousness," and all things become possible.

*God is with me.* I believe it implicitly.

Oddly enough, through all the times I have used it, I have yet to find evidence of prayer unanswered or God withholding any good from me. Instead, I *have* found, upon close examination when things have gone wrong, ample evidence of my own colossal ego having asserted itself and messed things up. Then it would produce all sorts of excuses for the debacle it had brought about.

Excuses must not be tolerated. Either you and I are on the right spiritual path, doing the correct things, or the fruits of our efforts are shriveled and poisonous. Just as the day follows the night, so must our experiences follow in the manner of our thinking.

Yet, how often we *do* kid ourselves; how often we delude ourselves; or, to put it more bluntly, how often we *lie* to ourselves. By doing so, not only do we waste our time, but we also get into mental muddles and do harm to ourselves.

*By their fruits ye shall know them.*

This is the test, the absolutely certain test. Either our prayers are scientifically correct and are producing the desired results, or we are kidding ourselves. There can be no excuses.

It's that simple.

\* \* \*

In analyzing what occurred in this instance we find that two things stand out with unusual clarity: First, there is the fact that *intellectually* the man knew about creative prayer; and, second, he was *emotionally* embroiled in his problems. This situation created a sort of civil war within him. His emotional turmoil prevented his making practical use of what he knew. It seems that for prayer to be effective there must be both intellectual and emotional acceptance. One cannot contradict the other or no results will be forthcoming.

This man's solution to his dilemma was by getting himself completely out of the way. He did know that there was a Power greater than he was, of this he was convinced. For him this Power had the ability to do what needed to be done. Without having any clear idea of a course of action himself, without at the moment even being able to follow through on anything, he acknowledged and accepted the fact that Mind does know the answer to every problem and that It was right then creatively active in his life and affairs. He gave up trying to mastermind his life and go his lonely way.

He removed all the verdicts of limitation he had placed on himself by turning to That which has no limitation and accepting from It supply to fill all his needs.

Regardless of the nature of the supply necessary for the solution of your need or problem, that supply is available from the Source that creates all good things. But the degree and the extent to which it becomes available to you depends upon the verdict you have reached as to its availability.

The verdict *you* reach, whether it be one of limitation or abundance, is what happens to you.

## CHAPTER II

## THERE'S A REASON FOR EVERYTHING

Things don't just happen, in spite of the fact that they often seem to. There is always a reason, a cause behind every event and experience in your life.

You say, "Sure, I will agree with that."

But will you still agree if we add that the causative factor behind your experiences, be they good or bad, resides in the nature of your own thought? This, of course, is a very blunt statement and needs considerable elaboration. But in the understanding of it rests your ability to have the right kind of things happen to you.

Your thought is the pattern or the mold through which the Power greater than you are flows into form and manifestation in your life. Your entire experience is filled with your creative thoughts which have become tangible. If you don't like the situations you may now find yourself in, a change in your thinking will bring about a corresponding change in conditions.

Sometimes it is not possible to discover that a negative experience is the result of a pattern of thought you can easily identify. But often, if you carefully check over the way you have been thinking you can pinpoint a relationship between thoughts of illness and illness itself, ideas of failure and actual failure. In other instances you will find that you have a complete warehouse full of negative ideas, ones that you have stored away now and then in your memory, until it literally bursts from overcrowding and overflows. When this point is reached you begin to experience results of the thoughts you have stored away and forgotten about which have now established themselves as patterns for your experiences.

However, you do seem to be in the favorable position of being able to change your patterns of thinking at any moment, being able to start to place in the warehouse of your mind an entirely new content of a more favorable nature.

When there is the desire to change from a negative way of thinking to a positive one, from undesirable experiences to the enjoyment of good ones, you may be able to do it suddenly or it may be a gradual process. You may have an adequate faith, belief, and conviction, something firm to turn to which you have been ignoring. On the other hand, if you do not have this it is often necessary to build up gradually to the point where you do have a firm foundation of faith.

Without exception those whose thoughts are constructively creative in and of their experience have complete confidence in a Power greater than they are, that It operates in and through what they are, that It always responds to their thought by manifesting in a manner that corresponds to the content of their thought.

The difficulties with which you may find yourself confronted today may stem from a long or short history of negative thinking. But it does not matter, you can win out, you can have things start to happen the way you want them to happen.

The story told by W. R. Miller[3] tells of a search for new evidence that would invalidate the sentence he was serving. He found the new evidence, and as judge and jury declared a new verdict and discovered a new life of freedom.

*The Evidence:* A life devoid of any real meaning.

*The Verdict:* A worthless existence to himself and others.

*The story of a man who discovered himself:*

> I spent a miserable part of my life wandering hopelessly in the deepest and darkest caverns of my own thinking. Though not insane in the legal sense of the word, I displayed traits of mental incompetence from the age of thirteen through the next twenty-one years of

my life. Intolerance, resentment, bitterness, egotism, and hate carried me to the gates of insanity or death. Until, in the final throes of expiration and mental oblivion, I cried out for God's help. This simple act of complete and final surrender removed the last barrier between me and awareness — myself.

My subjective desire for the good life gave me the strength to crawl to the only help my captive mind had left — to a group of people who had found the spiritual answer that could relieve me of my problem, restore me to sanity, and heal me of my disease.

They presented me with a simple program of education based on an open mind, self-honesty, willingness to learn, humility, and a concept of God I could understand. Through their teachings, fellowship, strength, and hope, my mind gradually cleared and I once again enjoyed physical well-being.

The healing of my mind and body progressed and I became more and more aware of this thing that had happened to me. I discovered one persistent fact: Guidance, right action, and corrective assistance became mine when I finally sought God. He could and would give me a life that could be lived. I had received training in an orthodox Christian Sunday school as a child and found it easiest to pray to the Father of my childhood.

My simple, daily prayers were being answered in a manner I considered miraculous at that time. Serenity, tolerance, patience, and understanding entered into my daily life, where depressive emotional turmoil had been present. Then I realized that some of my desires were being acted upon merely through the way I thought about them. Wishes and hopes were being granted without any audible or conventional form of prayer. But spiritual frustration momentarily overtook me as I realized I didn't know just what prayer was.

The Divine response to my simple faith released a flood of questions. Just how must I pray? What was correct? What was required of me after having prayed? Did God ever answer "No"? Should I accept adverse conditions as His desire for me? Was He a God of wrath and punishment? And as I wrestled these things around in my mind, I discovered that my former prayer of faith was also evading me.

One night I chanced to hear a man talking on our "common problem" who interlaced his remarks with scientific teachings. After the meeting I spent several hours with him and this conversation removed some of my frustrations. He pointed out that there was an exact scientific approach to prayer, there was a natural Law of Cause and Effect which, when properly activated by my word or thought, manifested a correspondence in my life. This Power had always been available to me, and gave explanation to the seeming miracle of my recovery. For when I had sincerely expressed a mental desire for the good life, the Law had responded and I was guided to those who understood my problem best.

His answers to my questions were clear, concise, and convincing. But being of an orthodox Protestant denomination I was wary of modern metaphysics. This was radical and not in keeping with my childhood training. He pointed out to me that science was not a substitute for my religion, but an aid to it. Nevertheless, I entered into another period of mental confusion. Could I accept this into my life? What would my family say? My friend prepared for me a meditation toward right action and guidance and instructed me in its use.

One night, being in deep thought concerning my decision, I spoke the words he had given me in all earnestness. Before I had completed this declaration, a childhood memory crowded into my turbulent mind. My grandmother had often said, "The answer to any problem can be found in the words of the Master." This was my answer. This was the mental guidance I had prayed for!

I took my Bible down from the shelf, blew the dust from its cover and edges, and let it fall open to the Gospel of Luke. Starting with the first chapter I began to read. My eyes skipped through the fourth chapter and I had almost finished glancing at the fifth when my eyes were drawn back to the fourth verse. I read: "Now when he had left speaking, he said unto Simon, Launch out into the deep, and let down your nets for a draught." And the story goes on that Simon Peter reported to the Master that they had already fished all night and had caught nothing. But on the strength of Jesus' word they would try again. And doing so, the nets became so full they nearly broke, and Peter called to the other fishermen to bring their boat and share in the catch. And both boats were filled to near sinking!

Bible students will recognize these verses as containing one of the greatest lessons in faith to be found in the New Testament. But for me they proved to be guidance for decision and courage in determining the spiritual course I should follow. The lesson in faith impressed me, but Jesus' words to Simon Peter were more significant. The Master's words contained the answer I had been seeking: Faith is nothing more than the courage to believe, to accept, use, and demonstrate God in our lives.

My friend, and the many I have since made, guided me in the application of this message. *Science of Mind* Magazine became one of my first textbooks. It led me to other reading material and to the educational facilities available to those who wish to sail out in deeper waters. To me, there is no horizon to spiritual awareness. The Divine Helmsman needs no star to guide by, for He is the Star. The voyage of spiritual unfoldment is a continuing journey of learning. There is no Port of Call, but merely stopovers to replenish my livingness.

Through it all, though, is one undeniable fact: Without demonstrations my "ship" becomes caught up in a calm. Had I not demonstrated my friend's prepared meditation that night a year and a half ago, I never would have put out from shore into the deep. I would still be frustrated over my small "catch" along the banks. Each demonstration, each fulfillment spurred me on.

Today there is no frustration, disharmony, limitation, or poor health in my life or the lives of my family. There is daily demonstration of abundance in all things. I am continually aware of the Life-Force within me and within all those with whom I come in contact. I know that as God is, I am. As God does, I seek to do. And as God thinks, I seek to think. My nets have broken from the weight of my catch.

The conclusion of the passage from Luke is also the conclusion of this article. No one can "sell" you this way of life; it is yours for the accepting. But I have proved that if with abundance I measure out true love, love is returned to me more abundantly. Peace and harmony, freely displayed, return to me in bountiful measures. And by demonstrating deep faith and courage for the inspiration of others, the Infinite returns them to me tenfold.

I now know that, among all men, I am most richly blessed. May you, too, know the depth of God's fulfillment in your life.

\* \* \*

# THERE'S A REASON FOR EVERYTHING

This story of a man who literally pulled himself up by his own bootstraps might be an indication of what everyone has to do from time to time. There are often helping hands but the actual doing each has to do for himself.

Regardless of who you are, or what position you may be in, every now and then it would be wise to take stock of what you believe in, and the way you are thinking.

Whether you happen to be familiar with modern metaphysics and the way of using the creative power of your thought, or are just new to it, there is always a need for a re-evaluation of your convictions. It is necessary to remove ideas that are outmoded, ineffective, and impractical so as to make room for those which can have a direct and practical impact on your life today.

As for those of you to whom the idea is new, the advice is to take it easy. Proceed carefully. One needs to have firm spiritual convictions. If upon close examination some of yours do not seem too sound — logical, consistent, and intelligent — don't throw them out until you feel you have something more worthwhile to replace them.

In the last analysis actually no one and no thing stands between you and your Maker. Life is expressing Itself in and through you, as you, and nothing can place a barrier between the two except you — by what you think.

You are the one who will have to take stock of the situation you find yourself in. You are the one who will have to determine what you are thinking. And most important of all, you are going to have to decide, arrive at a verdict, as to what you are going to think from now on.

If you decide you are going to have a better life and that is your verdict, then it can only be carried out, fulfilled, through the daily consistent pattern of your thinking. Your obligation is in maintaining the pattern. Vast new vistas of thinking and living await you if you dare to free your mind from the limited concepts you may have accepted from others or built up for yourself.

The fact that thought is a creative factor in your life and experience rests in the inherent nature of the infinite Intelligence of the Universe Itself — God.

You need to unfetter your thinking and allow it to soar, to be free to create new concepts of faith and belief in Life, God, and the Universe which can bring you increased joy and happiness.

## CHAPTER III

## THE PRICE OF HEALTH

Of primary interest and concern to you is the state of your health. Something is always happening to it. It is getting better or worse; it is never a static thing. It has a dynamic quality which is continually active.

You may be one of those individuals who is going through life with relatively few minor disturbances to upset your sense of well-being. On the other hand, it could be that you are constantly plagued with one serious ailment after another. In either case you want to be free of any and all physical conditions that might impair a fuller experience of joyous living.

Usual and proper procedure for anyone confronted with ill-health is to seek adequate medical assistance, of this there is no question. But regardless of what the physician may say, prescribe, or do, there still remains the fact that all that he can possibly do is to pave the way for the corrective, healing, and reconstructive processes of Life Itself. After he has done all that he can with his knowledge, wisdom, and skill, he must stand aside and let Life take over and express Itself.

Aside from some chemical or physical violence to the body the only thing that seems to be able to limit the degree to which Life may express in and through you is your own pattern of thinking! The doctors say that for a seriously ill person to recover there must be the "will to live." There must be an acceptance of Life, not a rejection of It.

You may well ask yourself just what kind of a verdict you have pronounced relative to your health. Have you mentally decided to be sick or well, to reject or accept Life? What you accept mentally you come to experience.

Every organ and function of your body is directly related to the brain through the nervous system. The messages sent out by the brain to all parts of the body are controlled, conditioned, or initiated by the pattern of your thoughts. What you think aids or impairs the normal natural functioning of every part of your physical being. Not only this, but the pattern of your thinking may so condition your body as to let it welcome or reject the invasion of infectious diseases.

The price you must pay for health appears to rest on three things: common sense in the care of your body; the decision, the verdict you have reached mentally as to what your experience of health shall be; and the ability to realize that in spite of what the evidence may be, what verdicts others may have reached regarding your condition, you may render a new verdict based on an awareness of new evidence you have discovered about yourself.

Anna Stoddard [1] had more or less reached the end of her rope. Every possible medical aid had been sought. She faced another of a long series of operations; this one she had little chance of surviving. There was no place to turn, little else that could be done. But deep inside her there was that inner spark, that will to live — Life seeking dynamic expression through her.

*The Evidence:* An irreparable physical condition.

*The Verdict:* The remainder of her life to be one of suffering.

*A story of health regained:*

> I paid the delivery boy the $6, closed the door and stood looking at the package in my hands. Then I quickly dropped it, unopened, into the wastepaper basket! My mind was made up!
>
> For many years I had not been well, and a major operation in 1921 had done little to improve my condition. In 1935 I woke one morning to find the incision had burst and bile pouring from my right side. From that day on for ten years I was to know only a daily dressing of an open wound, a series of different painful treatments and diets, and to hear the sincere regret

repeated by specialist after specialist, "I am sorry, there is nothing more I can do."

So in 1945, after six months of a very special treatment in a sanitarium, came the last verdict — another operation! Statistics showed that only three out of a hundred had survived such an operation. The thought that had sustained me in attempting each new treatment was: Someday, I shall be well again! But my body had not responded and I now weighed only eighty-five pounds. Another operation? The medical staff of the company where I was employed was eager for me to try it. I put off my answer.

A new search for a cure must begin at once! Where? How?

One evening in the midst of my desperate yearning to be well, strong, and happy, a long-distance call from a friend brought me great hope. He had heard of a way of thinking and believing that could change one's life, at least it had helped, in a wonderful way, the friend he was visiting. He gave me the names of two books and urged me to buy them and study them carefully. I could hardly wait for morning to come and the bookstore to open.

What a message of life and wholeness! They renewed my belief in health and happiness. My marriage had recently been dissolved and I knew the despair of a broken heart as well as a broken body. The days that followed in daily study of the books revived the expectation of joyous living, too.

A call from the company nurse — again I put off my answer.

About this time, I was invited by another friend to hear a lecturer who had recently come to our city. During the series of talks, he gave a prayer that I took to myself from that day on: "I am well with the Wellness of God; I am strong with the Strength of God. The life in me is God in me, and He makes me perfectly well, now." It literally became my "theme song." The words fell into a merry tune as I hummed them to myself throughout the days that followed.

The persistent periodic phone call: "Will you have the operation now, Anna? We must start making arrangements." Again, I delayed my answer.

Through still another friend, a magazine was placed in my hands. Day after day I read and reread its inspiring editorial until I had an overwhelming desire to talk with the writer, whom I shall call Mrs. X. I had never experienced such an impelling urge. I was still adhering to my prescribed diet, taking expensive medicine imported from Europe, and daily dressing the unhealed opening in my side. But these were days of great hope — more than I had had in many, many years.

So the arrival of the $6-package, a refill of my prescription of the pills I was taking, brought me to an immediate decision — I would go to the Coast and see that woman. "If two of you shall agree . . ." I had no sooner dropped the package in the basket, as an end to that kind of treatment, which I had followed for months with no apparent benefit, when the telephone rang. I patiently listened to the nurse's voice again advising that the operation be performed without further delay. I explained that I had decided to leave the state. When she warned that I would no longer receive the hospitalization benefit from the company if I took treatment out of the state, I was amazed to hear my own voice reply, "Just leave me alone! I have cooperated with every doctor and with every kind of treatment you have advised and now I want to try it my way. Put me through to Accounting, please." I asked that any monies due me in severance pay be sent at once, and I terminated my connection with the company where I had been employed for twenty-three years.

The amount sent was just enough for my trainfare to the Coast. I had no difficulty in giving up my apartment as it was at a time when living quarters were at a premium and the manager had a list of eager applicants. The next day I was on my way.

My sister lived in the same city as Mrs. X and it was to her home that I went from the train. While the trip had been without incident, it was physically tiring and when I arrived I fell upon the living room sofa utterly exhausted. Whereupon, my sister began pleading with me to consider having the operation. That word was like a battle cry. I found myself saying determinedly, "Just leave me alone, I want to try my way. But if it doesn't work out, I give you my promise I will do whatever you want me to do without further argument."

The next day I made my way by streetcar to Mrs. X's office. I entered with a feeling mixed with gladness and sadness: glad that the long-contemplated journey was ended; sad that for the first time in the years of sickness I actually felt my time on earth was nearing the end. The pain in my side had been most severe and I hunched over like a very old lady as I was led to a chair.

Then the quiet question, "Do you believe in God?"

"Yes."

"Do you believe I can help you?"

"That's why I have come all this way to see you."

The interview of forty minutes seemed like five! How to describe the confidence and faith of this writer and practitioner of the Word of God! The fears, the anxieties, the doubts, and resentments of the years of my life were as if washed away, and only the great Love of God seemed to remain in my heart. As I rose to go I was asked not to talk about my condition to anyone. The young woman was leaving the city the next day and would be gone for several weeks, but she said she would continue her work for me and gave me her address so I could write her the results. That was my only interview with her.

It is so easy to be voluble about one's aches and pains, the desperate lonely moments, the trials and tragedies of life; but where are the words to tell of the quiet, skillful mending of a body and of a life by prayer? Of a way so strong and joyous — and so painless? Yes, I think that was my very first realization, I had no pain! I stepped from the building tall and straight, my arms swinging freely at my side — they just didn't fall into the habitual protective cradle over my side. My side! Was that a quiver that ran through it? I remember saying, "Why, I'm being healed already!" And I strode off, walking the two miles to my sister's home with a strength I had not known for twenty years.

My sister asked about my side the first thing. I jokingly said, "Which side?" At dinner that night I ate a normal portion of everything, somewhat to her horrified amazement, for she had often seen me weigh every ounce of the few foods permitted by my diet.

The next day I sought employment at one of the branch offices of the company I had formerly worked for and was hired at once. Due to an overworked medical staff, I was not asked to take a physical immediately, though of course my medical records had to be sent for from the other office.

For eight days I felt as if I were immersed in a great strength and a deep inner joy, a wholesome quiet kind of joy that literally radiated through me. The girls in the office wanted to take turns sitting by me, because as each one said, "I feel so good when I am near you, somehow." What a contrast to a few months ago when even my close friends turned from me with such pity in their eyes! And my work was so easily accomplished. Nothing seemed to tire me. I was gaining weight, and my body was healing from the inside! The flesh around the wound had drawn together until it looked somewhat like the kernel of an English walnut.

On the evening of the eighth day I returned home late from an engagement and was hurriedly undressing when something dropped to the floor. "Oh, shucks," I thought, "a button from my suit." I picked it up. It felt like a piece of petrified wood and was about the length of my little finger. The kernel! I looked at my side. The skin was as smooth as the palm of my hand. Only a slight discoloration gave evidence of its having been there. The next day I popped the kernel into a little tin can and sent it off to one of the doctors who had treated me and told him to file it along with the X-rays, reports, and other data for that was the end of the case. And you can imagine the happy and grateful letter that was dispatched to Mrs. X. Four days later I passed my company physical with ease.

The year 1955 rounded out for me a full decade of wonderful health and a wonderfully happy marriage. Soon after my physical healing I had met and married the man who has truly been the kind and loving husband and companion I had so longed for. And while the great strength and joy of those eight days of long ago have diminished in intensity, there has been a quickening through the years of a deep assurance and steadfast reliance upon the great Power at the heart of my life — God.

To God all things are possible. And to you who may need a mending of the body, I say the *Wellness of God* is yours, for you are truly life of His Life, and love of His Love.

\* \* \*

Anna Stoddard walked out of her prison of ill-health a healthy and happy woman. Her escape was made possible not through any outward means but through the silent invisible activity within her of Life — God expressing His perfection in and through what she was. She did not and could not cause God to be more than He was, rather she accepted more of what He was. This acceptance was a mental act, a pattern of thinking that became a channel for a greater experience of health — that which is not a man-made thing but can only flow from the Creator of all good things.

You will find that for the most part you are not in the least interested in your state of health as long as it is good. However, the moment you start to lose any degree of it you become greatly concerned and start to do something about it. This everyone seems to do. But you are overlooking the fact that in order to keep and maintain what you have, you must do something about the keeping and maintaining of it.

Certainly you can do a lot of things about regaining what you may have lost, but why lose it in the first place? For the most part a loss occurs as a result of negative patterns of thinking which you allow yourself to indulge in.

Another story of health regained is told by Gus Goodman.[5] Again, in this instance, outside help seemed to be of little value. For him health began as an inside job. He had to rearrange his thinking.

*The Evidence:* Internal ailments.

*The Verdict:* No medical relief.

*The story of the evidence of right thinking:*

## THE PRICE OF HEALTH

As a small child, I believed in a Divine Power. I was taught that lesson by my mother, who was a devoutly religious person.

As time went by we children all grew up and separated, but the lessons I was taught as a child seemed to linger with me, regardless of everything else. I was always searching, seeking to learn more about our Creator. During the years, I was affiliated with different denominations and took part in their religious beliefs, but none seemed to appeal to me. I felt that there were great spiritual lessons in the universe I should strive to find and understand which would also enable me to have a healthier body.

My daughter lived in Southern California, and still does. However, at that time I lived in St. Louis, Missouri. We had been separated for several years. At last, I finally made up my mind to pay her a visit.

My visit lasted about seven months and I enjoyed it very much. We often had conversations regarding our spiritual beliefs and I discovered from our talks that we were both searching for one and the same thing — our relationship to God's creative Power. But we could not find the proper source. On leaving, I promised to return soon and spend more time with her.

Instead of returning, misfortune interfered. Four days following my return to St. Louis I was struck down by an automobile and was immediately rushed to a hospital in a serious condition. With my strong faith in a loving Father, and excellent medical care, I recovered unusually soon. During my time in the hospital I realized there must be a creative Power within me that gave me confidence and helped to heal my injuries sooner than was expected by those about me. But on leaving the hospital, I was confronted with the possibility of never walking naturally again.

For several years previous to the accident I had been troubled with indigestion, stomach trouble, and muscular rheumatism of my limbs. Following the accident I began to suffer more with my stomach and limbs.

My daughter also had been ailing for quite a few years with arthritis. She had paid out enormous sums of money for various miracle drugs, obtaining relief for only short periods. This was one of the reasons why I was anxious to return to her.

I was waiting eagerly for an answer to a recent letter to her. When it arrived she had written of a peculiar happening that convinced her that she had discovered what we had been searching for. She didn't comment very much on the subject, and I had no idea of what she was referring to at the time. My mind was mostly occupied with making arrangements for my return trip to California.

The time came for me to start the trip, and although my physical body was not in a very healthy condition I made the trip all right.

On my arrival I was standing on the platform of the train when I saw her walking toward me. I was very surprised to see the wonderful change that had taken place in her whole body in so short a time, and the joyful look on her face. On our way home I inquired what had made such a great change, and she replied that she would explain the next day. The next morning I learned all the details of the new discovery. Her husband's workshop was a short distance from the residence. There was an old family trunk stored in the shop that had not been opened for a long time. Here is her story of her find:

"It was difficult to walk any distance at that time, but something had been telling me to go and open the old trunk. I could hear those words again and again. I took a walk to the shop, opened the trunk and began rummaging through its contents. I noticed an old book in particular, published many years before, entitled *In Tune With the Infinite*. I began to study the contents of the book, and it did not take long before my eyes were open and I began to feel the omnipresent and healing Power of God.

"Then I began to search for a greater understanding of the nature of the universe and man's heritage. I soon found what I had been searching for for so long. I am now associated with many others who have found a better way of living, and I am no longer living on miracle drugs. I am now healed because I have used the Power, Wisdom, and Love of God to stop the dreadful disease of arthritis."

That is my daughter's wonderful story.

Although my daughter had explained to me her wonderful experience and how her health was improving, my stomach was giving me more trouble and I insisted that I needed to see a doctor. She was kind about it and made an appointment for me with the family doctor. I kept the appointment, but the doctor's examination did not reveal what was causing my condition. The next step in the effort to discover my trouble was a series of X-ray photographs, nine in all, and the diagnosis was liver trouble. The doctor gave me a prescription which I had filled. I took the contents without any relief.

Then I began following in my daughter's footsteps and studied metaphysics. In a short time I found the way to help myself in the healing of my body. Now I have gained a more satisfied mind and a happier life.

This law of healing I encountered was enunciated in the Bible by the writer of Proverbs who said: "As a man thinketh in his heart, so is he." As a man thinks deep within himself, so he becomes.

Jesus said the same thing in other words: "...as thou hast believed, so be it done unto thee."

Each of them was saying in effect: There is an area deep within man where the patterns of thought are formulated. These patterns are reflected in his life. Healing is often brought about by cultivating a spirit of love and forgiveness.

I learned that God is inborn in all of us. He is always ready to help us heal ourselves and overcome our difficulties in life. If we will only make known our wants and then have faith in our oneness in Him, all things will come to pass.

The eternal question which stands up and looks you and every sincere man squarely in the eye every morning is this: How can I better my conditions? That is the real question that confronts you and will haunt you every day until you solve it. The answer to that question lies just in remembering that the great business of life is thinking. Guide your thoughts and you mold circumstances. Just as the first law of gain is desire, so the first essential to successful living is faith.

Believe that you have — see the thing you want as an existing fact — and any right thing you can wish for is yours. Belief is "the substance of things hoped for, the evidence of things not seen."

\* \* \*

From these two stories you have seen that it is possible to regain health. Irrespective of how much or how little medical science may be able to do for you there must always be an active, constructive, creative pattern of thinking on your part. Without this, even the most skilled doctor often finds his hands tied.

## THE PRICE OF HEALTH

For those of you who may be ill there can be a brighter future. But before it can become part of your experience there must be an acceptance of it, announcing a new verdict for yourself. No one else can do this for you. You are the judge, and in spite of what others may say about you, you can declare that health, which is the normal, natural expression of Life, is yours.

The price of keeping your health is the conscious acknowledgment of it as the rightful condition of your body, and continually accepting it as your experience. Constant vigilance over your habitual patterns of thought is necessary either to regain or to keep your health.

## CHAPTER IV

## YOUR CRISIS FOR TODAY

You have often heard it said that the matter of everyday living is like riding a roller coaster. Very seldom does your day progress at an even, steady pace. Instead there seems to be a rhythm of high and low points. The high points may be moments of extreme happiness and the low points areas of critical emergencies.

The peaks of happiness are fine but how well are you able to face the crisis of the day? Do you have an inner assurance that you can face any situation, or do you give up, resigning yourself to experiencing an undesirable situation you would rather have no part of?

This does not mean that every moment of every day can be a moment of extreme bliss, but rather that when difficult problems or situations do arise you can do something constructive about them.

You are going to read about three crises which needed to be met. The situations could be entirely different for you, but the important thing is that crises can be effectively met. You can learn to meet them in your life.

These crises were ones that just suddenly appeared and something had to be done immediately, otherwise there would develop a long-lasting condition that would be far from pleasant.

Mary H. Boyles[6] offers the dramatic story of an event in the life of a friend, and it is the friend who is writing.

*The Evidence:* Fractured hip, damage to hip socket.

*The Verdict:* Probably never walk again.

*The story of appearances that were changed:*

> Mother was delighted — her very first formal wedding and a reception afterward at the town's largest

hotel. We left for the church with Mother looking like a queen in her new dress, hat, gloves, and purse. It was a beautiful wedding ceremony, then on to the hotel for the reception — and Mother slipped and fell on the terrazzo floor injuring her hip.

A doctor was called and after an examination his verdict: "Fracture of the hip with definite damage to the hip socket." On to the hospital and after six X-rays the radiologist concurred with the doctor and an orthopedic surgeon was called in. Mother was put to bed at the hospital, placed in traction, with the advice that it was necessary for her to rest for a few days, then more X-rays to be taken before surgery. She was 79 and the doctors were disturbed about her heart. They said if she survived the operation at all, it would be at least a year before she walked again, if ever.

Father had passed on a few months before this and we had watched him slip away a little each day for seven long months — and now this! I felt I could not bear any more. Down on my knees I went with a cry from my very being, "O God, help us, help us, I cannot bear any more."

Then a telephone call to you, my beloved counselor and friend, and your reminder that I was a metaphysician and the God who created that body of Mother's could also re-create. For me to start *knowing* immediately that God was in charge and that Mother moves "with the ease and speed and power of Light."

I went to my room for a few moments of quiet and meditation, and after awhile there was a certainty, the definite knowing, that God had taken full and complete charge of my Mother and I need have no concern — He was in His heaven, all was right in my world. A picture appeared in my mind and I saw a triangular-shaped opening in Mother's hip with small particles rotating and filling in that wedge-shaped opening in the bone — *God was in charge!*

Mother fell on a Saturday afternoon and the following Friday more X-rays were taken. In the meantime I visited her daily and definitely knew she was depressed. She wanted to come home, wanted no part of a hospital. She felt I could take care of her. The orthopedic surgeon called me in for consultation and advised there was one of two things that he could do. First of all he stressed the condition of Mother's heart and then said he was confident the hip socket was damaged, for she had no side motion of the left leg. He could operate immediately and put a plate in the socket and a pin in the fracture of the hip, with the possibility of her not coming through the operation; or wait for six weeks, giving her heart a good rest, X-ray her weekly, and then perform the surgery needed.

I explained Father's long stay in the hospital and his passing, and asked if I could not bring Mother home and take care of her, and then take her back to the hospital at the end of the six weeks for examination. (Knowing in my very soul there would be no surgery.) He agreed and we brought her home. In two days she was saying, and leaving no doubt in my mind, "I will be walking in a few weeks." I gave her the statement to use constantly: "I move with the ease and speed and power of Light." At the end of three weeks we brought her back to the hospital.

The verdict of the orthopedic surgeon: "Your Mother has a wedgelike fracture of the upper hip, and I wish you could read X-ray photographs to see how that fracture has filled in. Recalcification has taken place in her hip as it would in the hip of a youngster." The surgeon said if he had not seen the X-rays originally, along with the two other doctors, he would believe there was no fracture; but since he knew there was one he couldn't understand what had taken place. He said, "Take your Mother home, no more traction, put her in her own bed (we had been using a hospital bed) and I will see her in two days."

When he came over two days later he got Mother out of bed and we walked her around the room. I told him she could now move her left leg sideways, and he didn't believe me and had her move it for him. All he could do was shake his head, look at her and mutter, "I don't understand it at all." He advised that the following week we would start Mother on crutches, but Mother had other ideas.

Three days later, she commanded, "Get me a cane, you and I are taking a walk" — and *we did*. No crutches for Mother, no wheel chair, for she walks "with the ease and speed and power of Light."

The doctor returned a week later. "Mother wants to go downstairs. What shall I do?" I asked.

He looked at her again, shrugged his shoulders and said, "Come on, Grandma, we're talking a walk." Down the stairs they went and he sat her carefully in a chair while he dropped into another facing her and just shook his head.

"Here," she said, "read this. This is how I came downstairs. God walked me down." On the paper were the familiar words "I move with the ease and speed and power of Light." Mother said, "And Light means God," so there would be no doubts in the doctor's mind.

He shook his head and muttered, "I just don't understand." Then his face lighted up and he replied, "That's exactly how you came downstairs, Grandma!"

\* \* \*

You may or may not have encountered the devastating effects of a continually recurring headache or discomfort of any kind. Such a condition gradually wears a person down until life is hardly worthwhile, for there is always the fear of the next occurrence. No doubt a great contributing factor in such recurrences is the fact that you expect them to recur.

Marjorie Alexander[7] was subject to migraine headaches, and only those who have had them know the torture involved. The lesson of her experience can apply to most any immediate crisis that might face you.

*The Evidence:* Migraine headache.

*The Verdict:* Hours of excruciating pain.

*The story of a picture that came to life:*

> Any person who has endured the torture of migraine headache will recognize the symptoms. Usually following any nervous tension, fatigue, hurry or worry, a dull, throbbing head pain would develop and within an hour or two I would become so nauseated that the pressure of ordinary clothing would be too difficult to bear. My vision would become so sensitive to light that a dark room was a welcome retreat. Even my teeth ached. By then I would be lying as still as possible, fighting desperately to ward off the almost unbearable ordeal. The climax would be reached only after several hours of excruciating pain and nausea. Then the symptoms would subside and from sheer exhaustion I would finally fall asleep. Next day I would be very weak. This lasted only a day or two, then everything would be great again until the next frightening attack.
>
> I have said all that, to say this: After much metaphysical study I have found the unfailing cure for my migraine headache, and I firmly believe that what helped me can also help you who suffer in this way

Heretofore, I had taken every recommended medication without satisfactory results. During my first year of studying about thought and its effect in everyday life, I met with failure after failure to overcome this illness. But had I not developed an implicit faith in the infallibility of the Law of Mind I would have given up in despair long ago. To me, the study of this Law became increasingly logical as well as fascinating. I came to realize that if It worked for me in one instance, It could not fail me in any other instance — *if properly applied*. Finally, success came.

One evening when the old possessing symptoms began to take over, I decided that this time I would not fail; I would not doubt for an instant. It was a quiet sort of determination though, not fearful or anxious. I sat in my chair very still. I did not want to spend my energy in any way; I wanted to use my mind only. First, I did not tell anybody that I was ill as I usually did. Next, instead of picturing myself lying in bed suffering and trying to fight off my illness, I immediately formed another picture for my mind to develop. In two hours, I decided, I would be sitting just as I was now, but enjoying a specific television program in a perfect state of health. I held that picture in my mind for the two hours. Every time the suffering seemed to take over, and the temptation to crawl defeated into bed possessed me, I would renew my thought with the picture of well-being. Then I would repeat to myself that the picture in my mind must develop through the law of correspondence, and this law was infallible. Again and again I would picture myself in a perfectly well state within the next two hours. And I did sit, perfectly well, two hours later!

Now for a few specific ideas. Remember, the real fight is the choice between two pictures: The true picture of health, with every trace of the headache gone; and the picture of illness, the lying in bed with every unpleasant symptom present. This time limit is set by you. It can be anywhere from a few hours to a few days to a few months, depending on your mental capacity to recuperate. Let us say that the deadline for you is two hours from now. If you keep your thought steadily on sitting there well at that time that picture will develop. But if you let your thought stray at all to giving in, to getting into bed defeated, the illness picture cannot fail to develop. Your job, then, is to refuse to anticipate any but the completely *well picture*. As you do this, there will be a gradual subsiding of every trace of illness and within your specified time you will be perfectly well.

By my nine o'clock deadline that night I sat perfectly well and extremely happy. Happy because I came to know there really is Something greater than ourselves on which we can depend with *absolute certainty*.

\* \* \*

Accidents have a way of happening. You cut your finger, hit it with a hammer, trip over a rock, and encounter many other similar minor crises. There is also that group of people who seem to be accident prone; they are the ones who continually think they are going to have an accident.

The fact is that whether the accident is big or little, whether the verdict is that a life is in the balance or that a cut is minor, the same principle of action and the same process of healing is at work at all times.

The ability of the creative action of Life — God — to be immediately effective is demonstrated in Catherine M. Cates' story.[8]

*The Evidence:* A burned hand.

*The Verdict:* Days of discomfort and pain.

*The story of an immediate response:*

My neighbor and I were discussing spiritual healing. "Yes, it sometimes happens," she admitted wistfully. "But you have to be awfully good to experience it."

How wrong she is. I have experienced it myself many times; myself and those dear to me. And believe me, there are no wings sprouting from my shoulders! I'm no angel; far from it. But I've learned that Jesus meant what he said when he told his disciples that "What things soever ye desire, when ye pray, believe that ye receive them, and ye shall have them."

Up to three years ago my prayers had always been answered; but I never dared believe that God would answer my request for *immediate* healing. Sure, I believed that "If ye have faith as a grain of mustardseed . . ." But then I'd think, why should God do this for me? I've made many mistakes. I have so many faults, and worst of all, I'm afraid I haven't enough faith!

I would argue with myself; but I still wavered. Then one day in a metaphysical magazine I read an article about a little boy. He was asked how he healed himself and he said, "I don't. God does it for me. I say 'God, I don't know how; but You can do anything, so do this for me, please.' Then I tell God what I need. That's all there is to it."

Later that day I burned myself quite badly, so right there in the kitchen I said, "Father, I'm like that little boy, so excuse me if I don't know the right words, and forgive my doubts. But I know You can do anything and can heal this burn for me, right now. Thank you very much."

That burn was healed instantly even though it had been seared white and was quite large. That was almost three years ago, and since then I have experienced many other healings. I know that of myself I can do nothing. That God does it through me. And I know that He'll do it through you, if you just ask, believing.

Of course, we can't go to God with our hearts full of hate, resentment, or other destructive thoughts and expect Him to fulfill our desire for good. The only failure I ever had involved another burn on a day when I'd been wallowing in self-pity. And when I asked God to heal me I kept thinking, why should He when I feel so guilty and ashamed. Every few minutes I'd look at the burn. It took three days to heal instead of vanishing instantly.

So I know if we do the best we can to purify our thoughts and actions, then believe and accept God's help, we'll get all the help we need. Try it, and the result will amaze you.

\* \* \*

You can apply the lesson from these three stories to any crisis that might confront you during the day, whether it relates to your body or affairs. The point to be remembered is that something can be done immediately to correct the undesirable condition; there is always that Power greater than you are to which you may turn and accept an instantaneous response.

You will find that whether the results are fast or slow depends, to a large extent, upon two things: The faith and conviction you have in God — the Power greater than you are — to accomplish all things, and your ability to accept without any reservation the right action of that Power in and through the problem, condition, or crisis at hand.

In such crises that may confront you during the day you need to think clearly. Do not judge by appearances, but arrive at a verdict that is based on the best evidence you are able to present. Such evidence on your part would be the awareness that God's Knowledge, Wisdom, and Creative Ability are present

## YOUR CRISIS FOR TODAY

right where you are, and in and through what you are. There is nothing too big or little for God to do, there is no time element involved in His doing.

In your own thinking rests the only limiting factors in His action in your life and experience. You determine what is possible and impossible in your life. You are the one who marks off time, for in the Infinite there is no time, only the present moment.

You need to learn to accept *all* of what you may need, and accept it *now*, not as some future event.

In moments of crisis do not too hastily accept an unfavorable verdict. Thoughts are swift, so let negative ones go. Take a moment and turn to those which are constructive and productive of a salutary outcome of the situation — those thoughts which permit a greater experience and immediate expression of the right action of Life in and through you.

## CHAPTER V

## ASK, AND YOU RECEIVE

In spite of all you may think you know about the world you live in, the universe as a whole, and the infinite Intelligence in and through it, the chances are that you have not even scratched the surface. Regardless of how much you may feel you know about the nature of God, it only reveals the more that is to be known.

One fact often difficult to realize is that you are always, in some way or other, making a demand upon the Universe. Obvious demands may be illustrated by the snapping on of a light switch allowing the flow of electrical current, the planting of a seed, the eating of food. Each of these acts calls forth the creative Energy and Power that is at the center of all things, and there are definite results.

But there are other ways that you make demands on the Universe, ways that are not so tangible or obvious. Your thoughts are demands. A prayer is a demand. Such a demand is just as specific, just as sure of fulfillment as the fact that the light will light and that the seed will grow.

A number of years ago well-known author Larry Barretto and his wife kept a careful record of so-called coincidences in their lives during the period of a year, and which were related in an article in *Science of Mind* Magazine.[9] Upon analysis it was determined that neither chance nor luck was involved. Rather, each occurrence which might ordinarily be termed a coincidence was actually the result of a demand made in their minds upon the greater universal Mind.

Most unusual in their experience was the fact that the answers came in unusual and amazing ways. As a result it was often difficult to relate them to the original demands. In many cases they would not have remembered that they had made a demand

## ASK, AND YOU RECEIVE

corresponding to the answer if careful records had not been kept.

When you feel that certain things are matters of chance or good luck, if you but carefully examine your patterns of thought — the demands you have made on the Universe — you will find that you have received what you have asked for.

Just how such demands are fulfilled is impossible to determine, except that they are acted upon by a Power greater than you are, and they are specifically answered, but not always necessarily in the way or form that you might anticipate. Often such demands are fulfilled by the actions of people you know, and then again a complete stranger may enter the picture. On the other hand, you may find yourself assisting or doing a good turn for someone you know or for a stranger. In some way, without knowing it or realizing it, you become the channel through which the Intelligence of the universe fulfills a demand made upon It.

There are two people, unknown to each other, in the story told by Thelma Olson,[10] and each had made a demand, a request, on that Intelligence. They were brought together in such a way that each was able to be the answer to the other's demand.

*The Evidence:* Two people in need.

*The Verdict:* No visible solution.

*The story of "requests" that were answered:*

> We set the stage for ourselves all the time, but seldom are we aware of it. This is well illustrated by an incident which a friend once told me.
>
> "One Sunday morning a few years ago I wakened with an almost irresistible desire to play the piano," she began.
>
> "As you know, I am not a pianist. However, I used to like to sit at the piano and play selections for my own amusement. When my brothers and sisters and I were growing up we had an organ which we all played, regardless of our ability. It was our only source of music

in those days. My oldest sister had taken lessons and was able to accompany us when we gathered round and sang hymns and other songs. The rest of us were welcome to use her lesson books to help us learn the keys and notes. I later took piano lessons but never became an expert.

"On this particular Sunday I could not account for my desire to play. I had been away from any musical instrument for many years. My little apartment would not have held a piano. My radio gave me much pleasure and satisfied my desires for music and melody. As for wanting to play the piano, I had not even thought of such a thing in a long time, certainly not the evening before. I was amused and tried to laugh off the idea. But the deep feeling persisted.

"This was a very cold day with a strong north wind blowing. Instead of going to church I listened to several sermons and services on the radio. At noon I felt that I needed to get out for a little exercise. Also, I wanted to pick up a Sunday paper. I dressed warmly and went out to the street. In order to have a longer walk than just the short block to the drugstore, I decided to go to a store I had known a few years ago. It was several blocks away in a different direction. Upon reaching my destination I was dismayed to find the drugstore was no longer in operation. I was beginning to notice the bitter cold. I knew it would be wise to stop somewhere and get warm before going back to my apartment. But where to stop? I looked in every direction but could see no restaurants or drugstores. The closest one I knew of was too far to give me any comfort at that moment. So I kept on walking farther away from home, hoping to find some shelter before long.

"The intense cold was numbing my fingers through the thick woolen gloves. My feet already were like wooden pegs. I stalked along to keep up my circulation. And then I spied it! An open door in one of the little buildings along the main avenue! Through the doorway came the strong smell of kerosene. A woman inside was adjusting a kerosene heater near the window. Behind her were rows and rows of empty chairs. On the window was the name of a mission. I did not hesitate to go inside.

"I introduced myself and explained to the woman that I was very cold and would like to get warm before going home. She told me that the heater had burned too high and was smoking, so she was airing the room. She urged me to stay as long as I wanted to, explaining that she was getting the room ready for the evening services. She said that she lived at the back of the building; if I needed anything she would hear me call. With that she excused herself and went to her living quarters.

"As I sat there absorbing the wonderful heat, I looked around. The room was clean, neat, and orderly. And then I noticed the piano! There it was, the first one I had seen in months that was actually available for me to use. Feeling sure of her consent, I called to the woman; she came through the portieres at the back. She readily granted permission and brought hymn books for me to use. For half an hour or more I played, forgetting all about the cold.

"No, I didn't satisfy a deep yearning. That wasn't exactly the feeling I had. I enjoyed myself, although I realized as I played that I needed much more practice to play creditably. The feeling that gripped me was one of interest and joy to see how God had led me to this place where I would have a piano to use. As I played, I decided to leave a contribution with the woman, feeling sure she could use it to good purpose.

"When I was ready to leave, I again called to the woman and told her I was warm and ready to start back home. Thanking her for her kindness and hospitality, I offered her the $5 bill I had in my purse.

"Her face brightened. As she took the money she said jubilantly, 'God does answer prayer, doesn't He?'

"I rejoiced with her, and in answer to my questioning look she went on to explain, 'The rent on this building is due tomorrow and I did not have enough money for it. I have been praying since last night that the money would be provided. This amount takes care of it. Thank you and God bless you!'

"Her story prompted me to tell her that I had felt the need of playing a piano that day and had no idea of where I might find one. We both agreed that I had been led there.

"The woman then invited me to come back that evening for their services. She explained how various church groups took turns in coming to the mission to present services. She also asked me to stop in to see her any time I happened to be passing by.

"Because of the cold weather I did not venture out that night. On two different days I went back to call but could arouse no one by my knockings. I concluded that things were going well for her, otherwise the door would have opened again if we were meant to help each other."

My friend has a strong conviction that God takes care of His own. She said she had no compunctions about not trying to further contact the friend at the mission. Her desire to play that Sunday had been fulfilled; the prayer for rent money had been answered. Their desires had been accomplished. They

## ASK, AND YOU RECEIVE

had no claims on each other. Each was free to go her own way.

As I thought of the times I had followed my intuition I realized that wonderful adventures can be ours. We have set the stage and need but listen and act. "Before they call I will answer."

\* \* \*

Another unusual story tells of a long chain of events which provided a cumulative result. No one specific incident was a complete answer to the demand made.

Jane McLean[11] had decided upon suicide. For her there seemed to be no solution to her problems except to walk away from them. But in spite of her conscious decision there was an unconscious desire to live. In her case it was strongly enough implanted to constitute her demand, a demand that a Universe of law and order had no other choice than to fulfill.

*The Evidence:* A losing struggle to live.
*The Verdict:* Suicide!
*The story of a journey to freedom:*

> I grew up without any religious training. Oh, I said my prayers at night when I was a little girl and for a brief period in my teens I went to church occasionally; later I drifted away from even that slight acquaintance with God.
>
> Life went along. My grandfather visited me for several months and we had long talks in which he explained why he was an agnostic; I listened and agreed.
>
> Came the stock market crash, the depression; the end of one marriage, the beginning of another. Economic conditions worsened; we lived through zero weather without heat; finally we lost our home. I gritted my teeth and hoped. Things got a little better; we got a roof over our heads again. I started a business.

I labored fourteen hours a day, three hundred and sixty-five days a year for fourteen years. No vacations, no outside interests, no friends. After twenty years of marriage I found myself again in the divorce court.

Now I had a less rugged way of earning a living but I had monstrous debts. I struggled alone, eating the fruit of the tree of negation; frightened, lonely; the happy memories of a distant past blotted out by the overwhelming present and the years between. I contemplated suicide; fought it; looked at the future and decided in favor of suicide. I put up a cheerful front and began placing my house in order.

In the course of conversation with a friend I inadvertently gave an inkling of my intention. With disgust he said, "For God's sake, grow up!" I was stunned, immature or not, I did not care; sick and tired of pointless struggle, oblivion was for me. I planned to take my life late that night, but I stopped and had a look at myself first. I did not like what I saw.

Glancing over some books that same night, I picked up a copy of *The American Bible* given me by my agnostic grandfather in 1911. Thumbing through it I found a letter he had sent with the book. A charming letter to a little girl in which he advised, "Eliminate all fear, envy, and hate, and no matter if the way is smooth or rough you will always find a joy in living." The realization came that I was filled with fear.

I read *The American Bible* by Elbert Hubbard. I was interested in what he said of Ralph Waldo Emerson, Thomas Paine, and others. I decided to struggle on awhile longer.

I read philosophy, religion, psychology, anything I could find that gave me something to think about. It was tough going, with mental depression a constant companion, but I kept on. Eventually I read Claude

M. Bristol's *The Magic of Believing* and realized that as a negative thinker I was tops. Taking Mr. Bristol's words to heart I tried to change my thinking habits. I visualized myself selling property and paying off my debts. The first thing I knew I did sell a few acres; conditions changed as my mental attitude improved.

I got Dr. Norman Vincent Peale's book *The Power of Positive Thinking*. I realized Dr. Peale and Mr. Bristol were saying the same thing differently. I thought about well-known men that professed their faith: Lowell Thomas, Captain Eddie Rickenbacker, and others; intelligent men who had had great hardships. If they could believe, who was I to doubt? I began to wonder if a higher power was not guiding me. I realized that my unbelief could have been a contributing factor to the misery and hardship that was mine.

I followed Dr. Peale's advice. Peace came, followed by days of depression. I would go back to reading Dr. Peale and Mr. Bristol and after awhile serenity returned. Gradually the fits of depression grew shorter and less frequent.

Still not satisfied, I talked to others: Protestant, Catholic, Quaker, Christian Scientist. Perhaps I did not fully understand what they said, but I remained unsatisfied. I did not talk to any ministers, priests, or practitioners; I wanted discussion and opinion, not persuasion. Life continued to improve; I sold more property; paid more debts.

Then came the summer of 1953 and my first vacation in twenty-five years. I went back to a place I had always loved and to see relatives who were dear to me, but with whom I had lost contact for thirty years. All the way to Canada I kept telling myself not to expect things to be the same, but I could not discourage myself. As I drove into Maine, nearing the border, seeing the familiar countryside, I kept saying, "Thank You, God, thank You."

I reached my destination and found I had come home to a family that loved and cherished me. Friends living a hundred miles away dropped everything and came to see me. Young people not even born when I was there before, threw their arms around me and said, "We have heard about you all our lives." For three wonderful weeks I was filled with happiness. Vacation came to an end. I returned to loneliness, frustration, and anxiety, but I knew I was well loved. Looking back I can see God's hand leading me.

I faced the long winter and a lonely Christmas, but I looked forward to the New Year with hope and faith. Spring came and *Guidepost* Magazine had an article by Peggy Lee. Miss Lee, a metaphysician, mentioned Religious Science and *Science of Mind* Magazine. What did a metaphysician believe? What was Religious Science? What was the Science of Mind? I wanted to know.

I went away for a few days. As I stood in the Pennsylvania Station in New York waiting for my train, I was impelled to walk the length of the long room to the newsstand. I had a book to read, a heavy suitcase to carry, but something made me go to the newsstand. There before my eyes was a copy of *Science of Mind* Magazine. I bought it. The more I read, the more interested I became. I sent for *The Science of Mind* textbook. My search ended. With tears of happiness I found the Father that dwelleth within.

Peaceful, happy, free, and unafraid, today I have abundant life. I looked at myself and found God.

## ASK, AND YOU RECEIVE

O Father, bless the friend that told me to grow up;
but for him I would not have stopped to look.

\* \* \*

These stories point out the fact that even though we may not recognize it there is a Power that does act upon and supply the answer to a need we may consciously or unconsciously feel.

The important thing to remember is that, for good or bad, every thought is in some way a demand that you make, a demand that is automatically acted upon in a lawful and logical manner.

Considered from this point of view, just what can happen to you? Most anything! What kind of demands are you making? As judge of your life, what decisions are you handing down? What is the nature of the verdicts you are pronouncing for yourself that automatically become part of your experience through the orderly action of a lawful Universe?

## CHAPTER VI

## ARE YOU A STATISTIC?

One of the easiest things you can do is to recognize yourself as a statistic. Statistics are wonderful but who really wants to become one? Who wants to be a figure? Who, even if he tried, could become the average, the composite picture of some hundreds of thousands of people?

Statistics are fine for some purposes but not for you to hold up as the ideal picture of the life you want to live. No one can ever be the average person presented by mathematical calculation. One thing you always need to remember is that you are *you*, you are an individualized expression of the great creative activity of Life Itself. And the extent to which you let that Life express in and through you determines whether you become bound to the concept of what happens to the average person. (Actually, of course, there is no such person.)

In what respects do people unconsciously let themselves become the living embodiment of a statistic? Possibly one of the most common relates to ideas of old age. The records show that certain things happen to most people at particular ages; there is a time for the appearance of specific ailments, there is a time when thinking ability, eyesight, hearing, and other things begin to retrograde. But just who is "most people"? There is also the fact that many people go merrily through life without being in the least bothered by what others think and feel should be happening to them. They are being themselves and refuse to try to make their lives and experiences conform to a figure which actually has no relationship to them.

Such an unstatistical person is found in the story Grace Ware [12] tells about herself.

*The Evidence*: Advanced in years.
*The Verdict*: There should be a withdrawal from living.

# ARE YOU A STATISTIC?

*The story of what didn't happen to her:*

"I beg your pardon; I'm a reporter from the *Star*."

"Yes?" I asked, as the strange woman suddenly appeared at my side.

"I have been watching you play tennis. Would you mind if I write you up and make an appointment for you here with our photographer?"

"Write me up! a photograph!" I exclaimed. "No, I don't mind, but what for?"

"What for? Surely you must realize that you are a remarkable woman."

"No, I can't say that I do."

"But you run around that court like a young girl."

"Well, why not? I've been playing ever since I was a young girl."

"And still playing!" In her obvious astonishment I was equally astonished.

Right then and there she interviewed me as to my other athletic activities. And sure enough in less than a week there appeared in print, on the front page, a full-column article all about me. I certainly never thought my hobbies and interests would be of such public concern.

As a child I had always wanted to be outdoors playing games, doing the things my brother did. When snow came I was always in the vanguard, sledding down the highest hill, in the midst of the roughest snowballing, daring what any would; and accepted by the boys, for I could always "take it." Even during the blizzard of 1888 my brother and I had the time of our lives.

Through the years I have fortunately been able to indulge in and have time for outdoor sports. But for the last twenty or thirty years I have become somewhat furtive about what I do. Well-meaning friends and the few relatives that are left are constantly setting forth dangers to me, warning against such violent exercise. And I must admit their admonitions have often brought me up with a jolt, spoiling half the fun. My husband, however, was quite in accord with me, also loving participation in outdoor life.

When I was widowed, I felt a deep, deep loneliness which nothing could mollify. It was at this time I was guided into metaphysics and through it I have made so many friends I haven't time to be lonely. I love to be with these new friends. Not only are we of the same beliefs, but they are never surprised by my actions.

If I suggest sprinting down to the lake for a swim, they do not exclaim, "What! Drag ourselves back up that terrific hill? Oh, no, not me! You shouldn't, either." Or, watching me astride a horse in a brisk canter, they see nothing unusual. When I suggest a game of tennis they're quite apt to agree without further comment.

To them my numerous activities seem only natural: driving my car to the city night after night, to church and elsewhere through bumper-to-bumper traffic; finding time each day for some writing; caring for and walking my dog; looking after my apartment, cooking, and doing all the things that enrich life.

The teaching of modern metaphysics is always at hand to sustain me. I definitely, and for all time, refuse the verdict of doctors, friends, or anyone on age. However, I know that I must keep myself ever "on the beam," refusing to be alarmed by their warning advice. Let me give you a typical example:

## ARE YOU A STATISTIC?

The other day an old friend dropped in, starting the conversation in her accustomed way, "I do wish you'd take better care of yourself."

"Better care of myself? Nonsense," I smiled. "I couldn't be better cared for and protected."

"Oh, your new religion." She brushed it off. "What can prayer do for you if you insist upon abusing your body? Tennis, riding, diving, dancing, and all the rest, at your age! I never heard of such doings!"

"The world is likely to hear more of such things in the years to come, I'm certain. There'll be no old people. I - - -"

"I thoroughly agree with you," she broke in. "There'll be no old people if they insist upon going against all the laws of nature, vainly trying to hold on to their youth."

"Well, let's drop it," I interposed. "Each to her own opinion." I no longer tried to change her mind on such things. I'd known her too long and too well. *And he did not many mighty works there, because of their unbelief.*

But she was not to be put off, her "duty" unfulfilled. With a final fling she said, "Grace, I speak with authority. All the doctors — you surely cannot go against their opinions — tell us that violent exercise is very dangerous for anyone even twenty years your junior. There is always deterioration, lessening of physical power, hardening of the arteries, decreasing flexibility. It's only natural, like any other machine."

It was quite useless to mention that I was not a machine. I can only be thankful her plethora of negatives could no longer touch me.

"We must expect these things," she ended.

"We must expect" — with hurricane force this last phrase struck. Little did she realize, I am sure, the profound truth she had uttered. Those few words had cut straight through to the core of false beliefs on age, to all human woes. Some day she will want more out of life; something will awaken her to her Divine estate, release her from the necessity to suffer.

After she left I sat there for some time. "We must expect" evoked a chain of memories of aging personalities who had stood at the brink of despair, wholly unable to stay the final step — down, down to mumbling senility. Although I had done nothing for her, my own convictions were strengthened.

Are we not each a part of God? here to express Him unhindered? God knows no disease, lack, or age. Why do we superimpose on a perfect pattern the idea of fear, suffering, unhappiness? What one among us would willingly choose the "miseries" of old age to the wholeness, unfailing energy, joy of true being? Is it not as easy to expect the latter?

Instead of "declining years" life offers greater blessings, more understanding, wider vistas, higher horizons, keener appreciation of beauty. Only years truly lived can achieve such realization.

*Winter's furrows, to those aware,*
*Lead to a magic door.*

\* \* \*

Statistics show that for the most part today's business is so geared that things grind to a halt on Friday afternoon and do not start again until Monday morning. But in spite of this there are those who know that if there is a need, and a demand is made, business can keep going on over the weekend until the demand is fulfilled. A verdict that there is no more business to be done after a certain hour on Friday afternoon can easily be changed to one that declares that business is always available if you *know* it is.

## ARE YOU A STATISTIC?

The story told by Annie S. Greenwood [13] centers about a business firm in Minneapolis. It was conducted by a husband-and-wife team who knew how to pray, how to make their demand on the Universe and to accept the answer.

*The Evidence:* Close of the business week.
*The Verdict:* No more business to be had.
*The story of how a statistic may be refuted:*

> Leo and Ruth, Minneapolis mill owners, thought of business from the carload standpoint. That was habitual because they dealt in milled products which came and went in carload lots. Nutritional products for farm use constituted a large part of their output. Leo's insistence on high standards was a part of his religion. He considered that living up to the Golden Rule was more important than making temporary profits. His was the management part of the business; Ruth's could be called the "faith" part. They agreed perfectly and each augmented the other. Ruth kept the books and records for her husband. Together they applied spiritual principles and practices in all transactions.
>
> "You'll do your *work* on that, won't you, Ruth?" Leo would frequently say concerning some piece of business, as he turned his attention to the physical details of management, mentally alert, though well on in years.
>
> With serene confidence Ruth always knew that her "work" was already done. Her regular morning meditation, substantially as given below, had been happy and trustful, followed by right attitudes through the day's activities.
>
> "Father, I give thanks that this enterprise is an expression of good; that right action is the basis of all things and activities in this business. I declare blessings on everyone in it — our employees, all those from

whom we buy, and those to whom we sell. We do not want anything that does not rightly belong to us in the interchange of good will. We know that each one who deals with us gets his full measure of good; therefore we know that that full measure will be given to us also.

"This business is a channel for Divine Substance which flows to and through us and through the mill which grinds out our good. We give back to Universal Substance that which belongs to It. We do this lovingly and we are blessed for we feel the Father is keeping us a pure channel of right action. Because the thoughts of our hearts and the motives of our lives are right, we are blessed in all our transactions.

"We ask only what is for our highest good; that which brings happiness to us and to others because it is for their highest good.

"Father, I ask and accept that which is best and I give thanks for it because I know that it is done."

February, 1953, had been a slow month. Business in general seemed to have dropped considerably below normal. Other men in similar lines commented daily on the slackness of the trade and gloomily predicted another depression. When Ruth overheard such remarks or Leo repeated them to her, she would reply encouragingly, "Well, we're not in the red. We're doing a legitimate business; things will work out right."

It was Friday afternoon, February twenty-seventh, and Ruth was bringing the end-of-the-month figures into final order. An incoming carload of material from an adjoining state was standing on a local railroad siding, awaiting the bank draft for $5,100 that would release it, for their business was run on a strictly cash basis. Insofar as they could see, the car would have to be left there over the weekend. The workmen who handled the incoming and outgoing products had their work for the five-day week almost finished, but, as always, hoped that Saturday might necessitate extra work for which they would draw overtime wages.

Leo left his desk and came over to Ruth's saying, "If we could sell just two more carloads today we'd be all right. I know we're not in the red but this has been a slow month, and a short one, too."

Ruth looked up and smiled. Her faith was strong and sure but her thoughts turned to that waiting carload standing on the siding and she, too, wished that they had the cash for its delivery. It was afternoon, however, and she must close the month's accounts. In quiet confidence she turned to her books.

The telephone rang and Leo took the call.

"Hello. That you, Leo?" came the voice of a buyer for one of the local mills. "I suppose you're about closed for the weekend but I wish," he continued in the familiar vernacular of the trade, "that you could immediately roll me two carloads of 50% protein scrap meat, if you have that much milled out. Could you shove them in tomorrow?"

Leo assured him they could and would. Then he hung up the receiver and called across to Ruth the simple statement, "It works!"

With funds for the necessary draft assured, Ruth ordered the delayed carload from its sidetrack. The payment for the outgoing two carloads would much more than meet the cost of the incoming one. "It will be set in at your plant tomorrow morning," the railway official assured her. Leo told his foreman to have the crew ready for overtime work Saturday and to get those two carloads to the mill. The month's business was satisfactorily rounded out, with all obligations met and a gratifying balance of profit.

"Yes, it works," Leo remarked happily as they left the office.

* * *

A very popular statistical figure by which people try to regulate their lives concerns unemployment. They read figures in the paper about the number of unemployed people and then and there decide that there is no place where they can find work. And of course they never will find work if they are convinced there is none for them.

Another aspect of statistics relative to employment is that it is difficult, if not almost impossible, to find work after one reaches forty-five. Some people may not be able to find work at this age, and the figures may even show that most people are not able to. But the thing to remember is that you are *you*, not a figure. However, employment statistics will always be a very real and tangible barrier if you consider them as valid for you.

It can probably be safely said that it is impossible for you to adhere to any statistical figure *unless* you desire to do so. There is nothing in you that compels you to be the "average person" which is only a figure. However, you can have such experiences happen to you, you can become a *figure* if that is the verdict you pronounce for yourself.

In spite of the situation, condition, or problem that may confront you, you always need to remember that you render your own verdict, that you are free to either accept or deny the validity of any statistical figure pertaining to you or your experience.

## CHAPTER VII

## CALAMITIES CAN BE OPPORTUNITIES

How often do you pronounce a favorable verdict for yourself and then stubbornly refuse to accept it? The refusal not being because you don't want it, but because you don't recognize the manner in which it starts to appear.

As you look back over your life, no doubt you are aware of many instances in which you were literally pushed into some situation or series of events which were to lead to your greater good. Sometimes the pushing involved drastic actions to make you wake up to your greater possibilities and discover situations in which they might be more fully expressed.

When you declare a verdict regarding yourself, when you make a demand on the Universe, it is fulfilled even though the process of the fulfilling, in looking back, may appear to have been somewhat devious. But fulfilled it is, in the simplest, most direct fashion commensurate with your capability of accepting it.

If you come to recognize and accept the good that is available in every experience, it will not be too long before it will become apparent that "all things" do work for your better and greater expression of the Life that is within you.

Sometimes, if the heart is not too filled with bitterness and resentment, seeming calamity is actually but a steppingstone to greater achievement.

Many of the most beautiful architectural landmarks in Southern California are the result of the work of a man who was literally "pushed" into the best possible situation for expressing the talent he possessed. The route appeared uncertain at the time but the goal was there, not always clearly defined but inescapable.

The story is told by the nationally prominent architect Elmer Grey,[14] who had an inner desire to create buildings of beauty.

For him to fully express himself he apparently needed to be in new surroundings. He got there, and today tangible evidence of that inner desire may be seen in the Huntington Art Gallery, the Chemistry Building at the California Institute of Technology, the Beverly Hills Hotel, and many other buildings.

*The Evidence:* Physical breakdown.

*The Verdict:* The end of an architectural career.

*The story of the "push" that was always in the right direction:*

> In my early twenties I was practicing architecture in the city of Milwaukee and had planned several houses of some importance and a church of considerable size, when my health broke down completely. It seemed like the utter ruin of what had promised to be a bright career; but how often we hear of benefits that have come "masked as calamities"!
>
> A distinguished nerve specialist advised me to go to a sanitarium for a while, then when I got strong enough to get work on a ranch for a year or so; he gave me the name of one near Las Vegas, New Mexico. I followed his advice to the extent of going to a sanitarium, and finally left for the ranch he had named.
>
> Las Vegas at that time, many years ago, seemed to me to be a decidedly dreary looking town; and furthermore, I found that the ranch he spoke of was a so-called "dude ranch," where you paid something like $1,200 a year for lodging and the privilege of riding a saddle horse. These conditions appealed to me not at all, and also were way beyond my means. So I was confronted with a most distressing dilemma.
>
> Browning's words "Who never turned his back, but marched breast forward" came to my mind and I resolved, for one thing, that I would never return to Milwaukee with my journey West a seeming failure.

I had come that far to recover my health, feeling that it was a laudable purpose, and could not bring myself to believe that it should result in such failure. Is not a laudable purpose, accompanied by the faith that the God within us would somehow see such a purpose fulfilled, equivalent to a prayer, even though it may not have been put into definite words? My predicament at Las Vegas soon began to resolve itself.

I had left my baggage at a hotel and went to a bank to cash a check with the intention of getting out of the town and going somewhere — just where I did not know. But foolishly I had left home without an adequate letter of credit and the bank refused to cash my check, suggesting that probably the best I could do would be to wait there ten days while they wrote to Milwaukee and checked my account. Not a very encouraging prospect!

Greatly disheartened, I wandered about wondering what to do. Straying into a small public park, I sat down on a bench next to an old man, who I supposed might be an idle and unhappy creature somewhat like myself, and upon him unburdened my woes.

He heard me out silently for a few moments, and then, eyeing me critically said, "I have been a judge in this town for twenty-six years. Do you suppose they would cash your check if I endorsed it?" I thanked him so profusely for his unexpected and generous offer that finally he told me to stop — that I had said enough! It certainly was some encouragement.

However, with a check cashed and the money in my pocket I still did not know where to go. For want of anything better to do I walked down to the railroad station to watch the train come in from the East. When it finally arrived I was surprised to see a newspaperwoman whom I knew very well step off for a walk. Upon seeing me she exclaimed, "What on earth are you doing here?" Briefly, I told her my story.

Then she said, "I'm on my way to sunny Southern California, better come along!"

Instantly I thought, why not? So I ran back to the hotel, grabbed my baggage, boarded the train, and we were off! I have never regretted it.

After a few months spent on Catalina Island, fishing, swimming, playing tennis, and otherwise building up my strength, I noticed an ad one morning in a Los Angeles newspaper which read: "Wanted, a ranch hand in Hollywood. $25 a month and board. Must know how to handle horses." I certainly did know how to handle horses, horseback riding was a favorite pastime of mine. Furthermore, I recalled the doctor's advice to *work* on a ranch for a while. So immediately I crossed to the mainland, interviewed the owner, and got the job. The ranch was located on the corner of Hollywood Boulevard and Vine Street, not far from the Hollywood Hotel which had recently been built there; and its proximity to that hotel led me to become acquainted with its manager, Mrs. Margaret Anderson.

Much could be told of the amusing situations occasioned by an architect who was seen working as a "ranch hand in a black shirt and overalls" during the day, and in the evenings often donning formal attire and attending dances at a hotel frequented by people who were not accustomed to "ranch hand" companionship! But that is another story. Suffice it here to say that Mrs. Anderson, as well as some of her guests, were satisfied that I was not objectionable, and, although she had once known me as a ranch hand, a few years later she gave me the commission to plan

# CALAMITIES CAN BE OPPORTUNITIES 71

a much larger hostelry, the now famous Beverly Hills Hotel, the completion of which placed me solidly on my feet practicing architecture again in "sunny Southern California" and on a much more desirable scale than ever I had in Milwaukee.

What has happened in my life might well be described by some lines of Emerson's:

*Our helm is given up to a better guidance than our own; The course of events is quite too strong for any helmsmen, and our little wherry is taken in tow by the ship of the Great Admiral which knows the way and has the force to draw men and states and planets to their good.*

*Such and so potent is this high method by which Divine Providence sends the chiefest benefits under the mask of calamities that I do not think we shall by any perverse ingenuity prevent the blessing.*

\* \* \*

Along a similar line we find an experience in the life of Maxine O'Brien [15] which at first appeared to be all calamity, but which actually was the only means at the moment for her to be forced into bettering herself.

*The Evidence:* Forced to close her business.

*The Verdict:* Loss of income and investment.

*The story of a good verdict that was not recognized:*

> About eight years ago, after having been out of the business world for some time, I purchased a small public stenographic and notary business from an elderly lady who wished to retire and go to Europe.
>
> It was necessary to borrow the money in order to give her the price she asked in cash. I knew it would be a struggle until my debt was paid off, but I was optimistic and happy to be once again earning money.

My first problem came at the end of the first month. When sending my check for the rent to the building manager I also wrote a letter requesting that my name be placed in the building directory.

Early next morning I received an imperative call from the manager to come to his office. He informed me that — let's call her Mrs. Grey — was the tenant of the office, and if any changes were to be made in the directory only she could order them.

Explaining my purchase of her business only made matters worse. Under such conditions, he informed me, I had no right whatever to the office and they could not permit me to remain in the building. He said he had a waiting list of preferred tenants who were anxious to obtain space in the building; he knew nothing about me, and the building had a good reputation to maintain. I had no right, as he put it, to try to sneak into the building by buying my way in. Space in his building, he said, was not for sale.

He sat and glared at me while I stood on the opposite side of his desk and felt the tears coming. I had purchased public stenographic offices before, and as long as the rent was paid, a good quality of work and high standards maintained, no one had ever questioned the transaction; I had been considered an asset to the building.

I tried to explain that I had not intended "buying space" in any building; I had bought what Mrs. Grey told me was an established business. Furthermore, I had paid cash, and she had already gone to Europe with the money. My only way of paying off my indebtedness was to keep the location and build up her business, which was very neglected. The manager continued to stare at me silently as though I were

## CALAMITIES CAN BE OPPORTUNITIES

something that had just crawled from under a rock. Then he coldly informed me that I was not an acceptable tenant and he would require my office.

After walking the streets blindly for an hour I returned to the office, deciding that if he wanted a fight he could have one. Phoning several judges, attorneys, and well-known businessmen, I secured permission to use their names as references. Then I wrote the building manager a letter informing him that I had bought Mrs. Grey's business in good faith and it was necessary to remain in her same location in order to keep her customers; that if I was forced to leave the building and begin over in a new district the purchase of her established business was a waste of money. In this event, I would have to sue her for the return of my money, and of course would have to name the building in the suit. I also attached my list of references and an outline of my business experience.

A few days later I received a letter of acknowledgment from the building manager with the brief statement that the Board of Directors had decided to accept me as a tenant.

That should have been the end of it, but I had made an enemy — which is never good in business or anywhere else. The man never stopped trying to cause me difficulties. One time, on leaving a note on the door when I went to lunch stating when I would return, I was ordered, by phone, to the manager's office. He reprimanded me severely, saying that notes were not allowed on office doors (although I had seen them on several others!).

At the end of a year, I was handed a request to move, with the excuse that one of the tenants who already occupied one floor of the building desired to expand and required my office. It was interesting to note, later, that this tenant only occupied the office I vacated for one month, when it was rented to someone else.

All my business came from this building and its vicinity. There was no other office available in the neighborhood as far as I knew, and I had not completed the repayment of my debt. Moving was expensive, and to start in a new location seemed hopeless. What to do?

About this time I had seriously started studying Science of Mind. One statement hard to accept with complete understanding was that "the Law of Good is enforced in our lives." How could this be, with all my difficulties?

After pondering the fact that God does give us dominion over everything, the light suddenly dawned. *Fear,* and fear alone, was holding me back! Fear that if I left this particular building I would fail in business; fear that I'd find no other office space; fear that I'd lose all my customers; fear that I wouldn't be able to pay back the money I'd borrowed.

God hadn't given me the spirit of fear; I'd dug that up by myself. Spirit is absolute and unconditioned Good. There can be no opposition to It. It certainly wasn't the fault of God or Law that I had turned my back on infinite Good and persisted on staring into blackness.

With the change of thought came a change of situation. In an adjoining building I was offered not one, but a suite of three offices at less than I had been paying for one! This enabled me to sublet two of the offices to men who would pay extra for phone and secretarial service, giving me an assured income. I gained a new notary account which amounted to more

## CALAMITIES CAN BE OPPORTUNITIES

than three times the one I lost in moving from the old address.

Now, I can look back on a situation which seemed so serious and realize that *there is no opposition to Good.* Had I realized this before I would have saved countless hours of tears and worry. My present office represents a freedom as well as additional income, which I would never have known under any circumstances in the first location. I feel that I proved Good is All — and so can you.

\* \* \*

These stories illustrate several ideas which should be kept in mind.

Regardless of the nature of any undesirable situation you may find yourself in you cannot allow yourself to become involved in feelings of hate, resentment, anger, or fear. If you allow emotions of this type to dominate your thinking you will find it almost impossible for things to get better.

It is of utmost necessity to find, in spite of how small it may be, some good, some bright aspect in what appears to be an overwhelming calamity. The discovery of a plus factor becomes the foundation of better things that are to come.

It is wise to remember that all things can work for your greater good, if you will let them. Many times great men have only become great because of some seeming calamity in their lives. It was such an event that paved the way for their becoming the greater person they could be. You need to have this attitude toward all such events in your life. Otherwise you will find yourself buried in a mire of self-pity and negative thinking that will automatically block any future good.

There is also the fact that very often seemingly disastrous events are but the result of a demand that you have made on the universe for a better experience of living. The only way that it could be brought about was through your being forced out of one situation so that the better one could become possible. You had been blocking your own good.

When you seem to be pushed around, one of two things has occurred: It is either part of the process of the fulfillment of a good demand you have made; or it is the result of a continued pattern of negative thinking. In either event it becomes necessary to capitalize on the situation to the best of your ability and go on from there. Your attitudes and actions at that time determine the nature of future experiences.

## CHAPTER VIII

## YOU HAVE LIMITLESS RESOURCES

In all of the great variety and range of the stories you have encountered here, there appears to be a certain common denominator. Something happened to the people concerned, something flowed in and through them from a Power greater than they were. In every instance what happened, the action that occurred, was in some way initiated by the verdict they had pronounced upon themselves, the demand they had made upon the Universe.

The Power that does the actual doing — God, Mind, infinite Intelligence — is always right where you are. It is never limited, and within It resides infinite possibilities. There is a necessity on your part to recognize that there is such a Power, and that all of Its potential is available as you cleanse your thoughts and emotions of the debris which may be blocking a greater experience of Its good in and through you and your affairs.

There do occur those instances when the mind is free, when it seems to be unobstructed. At such times the thoughts soar to heights not usually attained. Some refer to these experiences as intuition, insight, or inspiration. It does not matter what you care to call them, at times a curtain seems to be raised and your mind is an unrestricted channel for its Source.

Such experiences may come unannounced, other times they may be invited. Receptive attitudes may be cultivated, but it seems that it has never been possible to deliberately command inspiration or intuition.

You may consciously relate yourself to this Source, and Its creative action as Law, by the means of prayer — the demand or the verdict — or unknowingly you may lower barriers to Its fuller expression through you.

Of unusual interest is the story told by H. C. Hand.[16] There is no verdict involved, no demand made, no prayer said. Something greater than he was announced Itself.

*Here is the story of his experiences:*

> There is a Presence with you now. How do I know? Let me share my experiences with you. Then you be the judge.
>
> What I'm going to tell you about is an experience that has occurred twice in my life. The basic principle is the same. However, one is aimed toward the material world and the other the spiritual, toward God. Both of these experiences, although they were many years apart, have a direct bearing on the admonition: "Be still and know." Both changed the course of current events. One changed the course of a world war, and the other the course of the lives of a man and his family.
>
> I was a radio operator in World War I on the *U.S.S. Raleigh,* patrolling off the East Coast of South America. We had been under way for several days. I was alone in the radio room and had been on watch for several hours; it was approaching 11 P.M. The night was calm and hot. The static in the earphones was like a thousand sheets of brown paper being crumpled, making the receiving of any signal next to impossible. Although we maintained a continuous watch, often days passed without a call for us.
>
> The rhythmic drone of the engine and the gentle sway of the ship had lulled me into a passive state of mind. I had been swinging the dial slowly back and forth across the wavebands, as was our custom, then for some reason I stopped at a certain point. I just sat there, pencil in hand, my log sheet before me. Unconsciously I had obeyed the admonition: "Be still and

## YOU HAVE LIMITLESS RESOURCES

know." I have no memory of how long I sat in this manner, but I slowly became aware that my hand, as though detached and independent, was doodling on the paper before me a series of short and long lines. I sat dreamily watching and wondering what was going on. Suddenly I recognized the short and long dashes of the Morse code. I aroused myself, alerted my attention, and was able through the bedlam of static to make out a faint audible signal from some distant station. Now this station was not "sending" in the normal manner. It did not have the customary brilliant rhythm of normal "sending" but was painfully slow and varying in pitch like a fire siren. It seemed to blend with the static. I would lose it, then have great difficulty believing it was really there. I wasn't sure of myself. It had been terribly hot. Could it be a figment of my imagination? So I made arrangements to take the same watch the following night. I had said nothing about what I had heard, nor made any entry in the log.

The following night I had difficulty in getting into the rhythm of the strange "sender." It was some time before I became aware of the same slow, siren-like signal. The alphabetic pattern was the same as the night before, but nothing I was familiar with. I concluded it must be a "twelve-letter code."

By now I realized I must report it to my radio gunner (warrant officer in charge). So I pressed the button for an orderly and instructed him to waken the officer and have him report to the radio room at once. I now believed I had something upon which he should pass judgment. On his arrival he put on duplicate phones and listened attentively, but was unable to hear the signal of which I had become so keenly aware. I tried over and over to explain to him that this signal was different from any he had ever heard before, that it was not being sent in the same tempo he had expected. It was all so different and difficult to explain. He would patiently try again, then shake his head and say I was imagining things. I begged him time and time again to forget what he knew and watch my hand to get the rhythm. I think it was only my sincerity and persistence that kept him trying. I was excited, grateful, and almost in tears when he got the rhythm of the signal and began to copy with me. He soon knew that it was not our code nor our Allies', but a German one. Realizing its importance, action was taken to get this information into the hands of Naval Intelligence in Washington.

It was many months later that I learned the story of how they traced this station and arrested the two German spies in one of our stations. They had been sending information about our troop and ship movements to Germany for many months undetected; through a very ingenious system which had blended their signals into the atmospheric noises detection was improbable.

Happy as I am in having had a part in this unusual experience, the following incident is far more dynamic to me than the picking up of this strange signal. I didn't realize then that some twenty years later I was to have a similar experience but in a different way.

I had received a medical discharge from the Navy, married, and returned to my home town to join my adoptive parents in business, only to give up dissatisfied. I received an appointment as a Federal Agent and worked as such for three and a half years, resigned and returned to radio, but left it because of failing health. I drifted from one thing to another until finally I was completely broken in health, heavily in debt, without a job, with a wife and four children (one of

## YOU HAVE LIMITLESS RESOURCES

them a blue baby). Each of the children had taken his turn at diseases, including scarlet fever. Everything seemed to be against me.

As a babe my mother had left me in an orphanage, to quote her, "to die." There were many times during this period when I wished I had died. My mind was filled with resentment, hate, fear, and problems. I had lost faith in myself, man, woman, child, and God. I was hopelessly lost in despair and self-pity. My wife and family were in as sad a state, and expected little from me.

Then it happened! One hot summer day I was given a shovel and assigned to a fire patrol in the hills surrounding Oakland. For me this was no easy task. I was sick, undernourished, discouraged, and so weak I often had to lie down to regain strength enough to walk a block. This day was little different from others as I struggled to the summit and sank down under an oak tree in welcome shade. Exhausted, I laid my shovel beside me. I was alone. I just sat. There was only the deep stillness of the lonely countryside, the stifling heat of a midsummer day, and the muffled rumble of the distant city. I merely sat there, letting one thought drift to another, not really caring. My eyes were open, but I was not interested in the dry sun-baked grass nor the dust-covered shrubs and trees below me. I don't recall how long I sat in this manner, nor do I remember any of the things I may have had in mind. I was in a passive, disinterested state.

Suddenly, I was not asleep, yet it seemed as though my consciousness, freed from the bondage of human entanglements, had risen into the clear pure realm of universal ideas; I seemed to be in harmony with the Infinite. I was as conscious of the ideas set before me as I had been of the doodling that night years before.

Idea after idea flowed before me, unfolding in normal, natural sequence of interrelated principles of universal importance to God and man; and man's relation to the whole. Everything was in its right place, doing its right work, and each was an integral part of the whole. It was like being taken behind the scenes of life and being shown the great Principle underlying all creation. I was shown the workings of the *eternal now*.

All tension left my body. A great peace came over me. I had a deep sense of understanding and love, with an all-inclusive sense of forgivingness.

I could tell you much, much more of what was unfolded before me as I sat there, and of the months that followed, of little children who ran after me, throwing their arms around me, saying, "I love you"; of those who stopped me to tell me my face shone like a smiling sun, and asked my religion. But the important point is that all the time I had been sick, poverty-stricken, tense and discouraged, there had been a Presence with me. Through all that backwash of my human woes there had been this wonderful Presence. If someone had told me this, I doubt if I would have believed him. Yet, up there on the hills, I had suddenly become aware of something new and wonderful. Something different from anything I had ever experienced before. Something that was to change my life and that of my family from want, sickness, and discouragement (not without some sweat, tears, and toil) to health, work, and a home of our own, with the assurance that there was an ever-present help for our every need, and always right where we are and when we need it.

Many people spend a great portion of their lives pursuing religion, reading many books, and counseling with teachers, hoping to find some mystical person or thing that will put them into the "secret place" with God. Hearing of someone's spiritual advancement they exclaim, "Oh, he is endowed by God; he has some gift we don't have." This is not true, for it was only by chance, as far as I was concerned, that I became aware of that radio signal, and here again by chance aware of the Presence. Call it Divine guidance if you will, but the fact remains that I had been previously unaware in both cases that such a signal or the Presence existed.

I believe that these two experiences make that point clear and should encourage all who read of it to seek diligently to quiet the inner turmoil, that they might recognize their spiritual heritage within themselves and depend on it in every phase of their lives. Books, religions, and loving teachers can only bring us to this door. It is we who must find the Presence within and contact It.

Intermingled in the inner confusion there is a Presence awaiting our recognition, whether we are in hopeless despair or in peaceful stillness and quiet. There is a guiding, blessing Presence, identified and unified with the universal One, for each and every child of God. Your mustard seed of faith will reveal It.

Divine guidance is always available to us. But for it, my warrant officer might never have heard that odd and unusual signal that night and the course of a war might have remained unchanged. But for it, my family and I might not have known the deep joy and richness of life.

\* \* \*

It must always be kept in mind that neither you nor any person of himself has the ability to create a moment of unusual insight, to heal a physical condition, or establish harmony in a confused situation. Rather, the establishment or creation of such favorable events seems to rest completely in your ability to make yourself a channel through which they may come to pass. There is a need to cease obstructing the action of Life in and through you. You need to accept more of what Life has to offer rather than limiting your experience of It.

For the most part people seem to battle against their own good. They wage the battle with negative thinking and destructive emotions. They seem to overlook the fact that Life — Mind, Intelligence, God — is good, creative, and constructive. A fuller experience of Its nature can only become a part of your life as you get your petty limited thoughts out of the way.

Joyous living, in any respect, whether it be in connection with your health, affairs, or relationships, can only come through aligning yourself with infinite Intelligence — God.

You can continually pronounce a verdict that will enable you to more and more partake of God's nature. You can make a demand on the Universe that will be fulfilled by a greater experience of all the good things that Life holds.

Many wonderful things can happen to you through the limitless resources of God.

## CHAPTER IX

## THE WAY THINGS HAPPEN

In considering all the stories you have read concerning favorable developments in certain aspects of living, you discover that it was a process of thought through which such events came about. Such thought may be considered as affirmative prayer, creative thinking, or positive thinking. It is in your thinking that you establish a verdict about yourself; it is in your thinking that you make your demand on the Universe; and it is only in your thinking that you are able to accept and experience the result. The necessity to think in a constructive and affirmative manner is obvious.

Your thoughts are always creative, whether they are for your good or detriment. But it is always to be remembered that your thinking is not creative in and of itself. It but acts as a valve which may open the passageway for the influx of that Power greater than you are, which can and does do all things. For you to experience the fact that there is such a Power in the universe there must first be the faith and conviction that It does exist. Otherwise how could it be possible for you to accept something which you deny?

The only way to prove for yourself whether your faith in such a Power is effective is to so exercise that faith that something happens objectively as a result of it. Something must happen to you!

The pattern of your thinking is evidence of what you have faith in. The response of the Power greater than you are can only be in terms of corresponding to that faith, to that pattern of thinking.

If nothing happened when you had faith, when you prayed, when you were convinced beyond all doubt that things were all right in your world, then such a way of thinking would be but a sort of daydreaming, a futile hope, an idle wish. But you have discovered that favorable things do happen as a result of constructive thinking. Similarly you can have them happen in your experience.

Why can such things occur? Why can dynamic creative thought produce a definite and specific result for yourself or someone else? Because there is a Power, an Intelligence, a Creativity in the universe that responds to you — a Power that *is* greater than you are.

Now where do you think this Power could be?

An ancient Chinese fable says that when the gods were making the earth they had a conclave to decide what they should do about hiding man's Divinity from him. They wanted to make him a Divine being so that he would live forever, but they wanted him to discover it through experience, as he was to discover everything else. One of the gods suggested that they hide man's Divinity high in the heavens. But another more experienced god said, "No. The time will come when man will perfect an instrument and he will fly through the heavens and discover his Divinity. Let us hide it deep in the sea." Another god said, "No. Man will devise a way to go under the sea and discover his Divinity. Let us hide it in the earth where he will never find it." And another god said, "No. We are giving man the capacity so that some day he will bore through the earth and then discover his Divinity." They finally called in the wisest of all the gods and asked of him, "Where shall we conceal man's Divinity?" And the wisest of all the gods said, "Conceal his Divinity within himself, because this is the last place he will ever look for it." And so they hid man's Divinity within himself.

This fable, like so many others, teaches a great lesson about life.

Whatever you may think faith is, whatever you consider prayer to be, it can only be something that you do within your own consciousness. It is only you who can have the faith, who can do the praying. And although you do this in your own consciousness you feel it has a relationship with something greater than yourself.

Faith can only start within yourself. (That is also the place where doubt and fear arise.) Faith, being nonphysical, has to be mental. If you did not have a conscious mind you would not be able to pray affirmatively, to render verdicts about yourself, or accept and experience the answer or response to such a process of thought.

What constitutes a thought of faith? Faith is the opposite of fear, it is affirmative. The faith you need to exercise, if it would be effective, is like planting a seed — you place it in the ground and have the conviction that something is going to result. Faith needs to be as simple as that.

Faith is also an acceptance, for you are accepting that good is either coming to you or is being withheld from you. Faith is not a generalization; it is not just a statement. Like any other of your thoughts, faith has to be in something, about something, to something, or for something. It has to be located; therefore your faith, like your thoughts, can only be right where you are.

Your faith, your convictions, your verdicts, your demands on the Universe must be of an affirmative nature, and definitely stated for a specific purpose, if they are going to be of value and cause something good to happen to you. If you went into a grocery store to buy a can of peaches, you would not walk aimlessly about muttering to yourself something about needing groceries. Instead you would state that you wanted to buy a can of peaches.

An active creative faith is an affirmation, a definite statement about something, and equally an acceptance that the thing stated will be accomplished.

You may ask, "How can I know that I can use a Power greater than I am?" You are doing it all the time — every time you plant a seed, every time you snap the light switch, every time you take a breath to sustain the life in your body. You use a

Power greater than you are every time you make use of a law or force in nature. You are always making use of a Power to which the united intelligence of the entire human race is as nothing.

But for the most part, when people come to the point of using in spiritual things the faith they have in everyday things they seem to get all mixed up. They feel that things termed spiritual are in no way related to ordinary living. Or that there are some people who know something special, or are better than others, or who have privileged access to God.

Who is there living for whom the sun does not shine? Who is there living upon whom the rain will not fall? Who is there living for whom the wind will not blow? All too often people think that Divine Power is only for someone else, not for them. But this is not true. The good things you desire can happen to you, can become part of your experience. And the Power greater than you are will not ask you whether you are Jew or Gentile, Catholic or Protestant.

You, and all people, are surrounded by and immersed in the miracle of Life. Life that you do not know how to create, yet you are living It. Therefore you must believe that right where you are is the *thing* that responds to your acceptance of the faith you declare, the thoughts you think, your verdicts and your demands.

It is the very simplicity of the whole thing that is so elusive. Don't go around looking for long-drawn-out, difficult answers and asking what the great philosophers think. The important question, and one only you can answer for yourself, is what do *you* think? No one can live for you. No one can think for you. You live with the God you believe in, believe in *within* yourself; and in this inward awareness you are alone with the only Power there is!

When your declaration of faith is consciously, definitely, and intelligently used for specific purposes of good, you have every right to expect something to happen, *if you do not in the mean-*

*time deny what you have affirmed.* This is probably the greatest stumbling block of all. It certainly is not easy to avoid.

Perhaps you have faith in something, affirm something, accept a new verdict for yourself, but then it appears as though it were not going to happen. Then is the time to *continue to know* that you are dealing with an Intelligence that causes the invisible to become visible, and responds in accord with the nature of that which you have affirmatively prayed for.

Thought forms a pattern through which the creative forces of the Universe operate in your experience. Your thoughts create the patterns of your life and experiences. It is done unto you as you believe — this is one of the greatest ideas man has ever discovered. But for the most part man has overlooked its full meaning. Jesus not only said there is a Power that *can* do it and *will* do it, but It *must* do it. But he stipulated it is done unto you *as* you believe. You do not need to ask anyone else for your authority to think, you *do* think. And if you want to find out if your thinking is creative, if your faith is effective, if favorable things can happen to you, there is no other way in the world to prove it than by starting to think in a constructive, affirmative manner. Then you will see the results. You will know the answer.

This Power must find a partnership within you, an acceptance within you, a belief in It beyond everything that denies It. Then at last you will be able to look at the rising sun and say, "It is going to be a good day," and to the setting sun, "I thank God for this day that has been good."

## CHAPTER X

## IT *CAN* HAPPEN TO YOU!

You have encountered much evidence *about* things that can happen to you, but you probably want to know more about the actual procedure by which you may actually have them happen to you.

No one can tell another how to think, how to pray. There are no hard and fast rules which if adhered to will guarantee results. But there are certain mental and emotional attitudes which may be adopted, and certain procedures which if followed may be productive of salutary results. Of this there is no doubt. They have been proclaimed for ages, and are being proved daily in the lives of thousands of people around the world.

Considered in this respect it can definitely be said that there is a science of prayer, which when properly applied will work for you.

If there is such a thing as spiritual Power in the Universe, It must work mechanically; It must work as Law. The mechanics for Its operation already exist; Law exists and we merely use It. All is a matter of law and order, not chaos, confusion, and whimsy. This is in keeping with all that has been ascertained about the world in which we live.

Everything that is known about our world shows that it is a unity, that its operation is in accord with law, and that there is in, through, and behind it an infinite Intelligence. You are a part of It, immersed in It, not separate from It. As such you are subject to, and avail yourself of, Its creative activity.

If people feel some prayers are answered and others are not, the fault lies not in the failure of God to respond in the manner we think He should, but rather in the nature of the prayer. The action which follows as a result of prayer is always a response which corresponds to the initiating factor — the thought content of the prayer.

In this respect prayers of supplication and petition, although they may be of value for many people, nevertheless would appear to be contradictory to the concept of a universe governed by Intelligence and Law. There is no need to ask God to be God. What needs to be done is to make your demand, to affirm the good you desire, to declare that what you desire to have happen to you is now happening.

All of this is but a dynamic understanding of the truths that Jesus proclaimed to the world, but which the world even yet but little understands: ". . . behold, the kingdom of God is within you"; "I and my Father are one"; ". . . what things soever ye desire, when ye pray, believe that ye receive them, and ye shall have them"; ". . . as thou hast believed, so be it done unto thee." These and many other of Jesus' words reveal a positive, affirmative attitude toward Life and God. There was nothing wishy-washy about his thinking, no doubts, no wonderings about the response that would be forthcoming from his clear and affirmative demands on and acceptance from the Power greater than he was.

There may be a need to change some of your concepts which are contradictory to what has been learned about the nature of the world about you — a need to change some of your ideas which are fraught with superstition, that verge on the edge of a belief in magic, or that maintain that there is something, or somebody, that acts as an intermediary between you and God.

If you consider that the Power behind the universe is Intelligence, that It operates in, through, and as Law, then it must follow that you must use It through understanding It, or in ignorance misuse It.

Your prayer that accepts its own answer complies with a law of the universe. Why? Because that is the way the Universe is organized, that is Its nature. It could not be otherwise and remain self-existent. You are dealing with a natural, spontaneous Power that all you can say of It is, "It is." All you can say of Its operation is, "This is the way It works." When you cooperate with It, then Its Power and Energy are available to you. An old saying is: Nature obeys us as we first obey it. Every scientist knows that he must adhere to the laws governing the principles he utilizes or nothing will happen.

The simple fact has to be faced that the nature of Reality is such, the nature of God is such, the nature of the Law of Being is such, that in some way, whether you understand it or not, you are so much a part of Reality that your thoughts, while they are not creative *of themselves,* are creative because they deal with a *creativity* that resides at the heart of Life.

Therefore, those thoughts which are affirmative, those thoughts which embody and accept, are like the creative thinking of God who cannot conceive anything other than Himself. In such degree as you assume this affirmative attitude toward the Universe and embody the meaning of goodness, wholeness, and beauty you will be able to partake of them.

People mostly seem to be able to touch only the outermost rim of the Power greater than they are. Otherwise, they would all be able to say to the paralyzed man, "Get up and walk." But the fact does remain that as you bring yourself more and more into agreement with Life, and recognize that the material world is not an illusion but, in a very real sense, is a substance cast in and as your experience according to the nature of your thinking, then you realize that there is a self-determination within Life which makes it move, and be moved upon.

In all your endeavors in affirmative prayer, in bringing to pass in your experience the good things you desire, there is one salient point to be remembered: There must never be a conflict between the intellect and the emotions, between the mind and the heart. Otherwise what one affirms the other denies, and no results will be forthcoming. You cannot exist as a house divided against itself. There must always be a unanimity of knowledge and belief.

So much for the attitudes which appear to be conducive to the establishing of favorable happenings in your life. As for the procedures relative to effective prayer, any suggestions in this connection must be considered as general guides only. They are merely signposts which you may follow. Just as others have taken them and adapted them to their own particular way of thinking, so can you. But regardless of the fact that they are to be considered only as guides, they have proved to be the salient factors in most prayers that have been answered.

The four factors which seem to be of utmost importance may be designated as Recognition, Identification, Declaration, and Acceptance.

> *Recognition.* This initial step involves a recognition of the fact that there is a Power greater than you are. That there is God, Intelligence, Mind that is in, through, and behind all that is. Within It is contained all possibilities. It is good and constructive. A thought in the Mind of God becomes tangible creation in accord with His action as Law.
>
> *Identification.* You need to know that you are a creation of God. God has become what you are through His creative activity. You are not a thing apart from God. You do not have to search for God, but rather need to become aware of the fact that the "Father" is within you. You, through your ability to think, through the creative power of your thought, are an active cocreator with God. You are part of that which God has created and therefore must of necessity partake of the nature of That which created you out of Itself.
>
> *Declaration.* It is at this point that you definitely and specifically affirm the good you desire. You establish in your mind the form or pattern of thought upon which and through which the Law of Mind flows into tan-

gible manifestation in your experience. The words you speak, the thoughts you declare as true about yourself, or another, must be backed by complete intellectual and emotional conviction. This is the constructive, creative portion of your prayer. This is the point where you firmly implant in the content of your thought the complete concept of those things which you would have happen to you. You ignore unfavorable appearances and affirm the good you desire. You render a new verdict for yourself. There is no wishing, hoping, or begging involved, instead there is a calm assurance that the word of good you speak is God declaring Himself in and through you and that this word is the pattern for your experience.

*Acceptance.* After a declaration there must always be an acceptance. To have, you must accept. You must affirm that the good you have declared for yourself is now *yours*. And of utmost importance, that it is yours *now*. Not at some future time, an hour, a day, or a year from now, but *now*. The only time that you can ever experience anything is the present moment. So you must believe that you have your good now. Although it may not appear as a tangible reality in your experience right this moment, the only way it ever can come to pass is to accept it as a present reality in your thought. And in the acceptance of that for which you have prayed here is the obvious necessity and desire to express gratitude and thanks to God that it is now yours.

You have read about many things which have happened to other people. You have evaluated these events. You have discovered a reason for their occurring, and determined what it was that caused them to come to pass.

## IT CAN HAPPEN TO YOU!

And here at the very last you have encountered the salient factors involved in causing such things to come to pass.

Little remains to be said, for the rest is up to you.

To the extent you are able to align yourself with the nature of things as they are, with the Harmony, the Good, and the Intelligence of that Power greater than you are — God — and Its creative action as Law, you will be able to have the good things you desire happen to you. If you seem to have a problem in achieving this goal, the difficulty is not with God, but with your thinking about God, and this you can do something about. Others are doing it all the time, and so can you.

This moment can be the start of a more wonderful experience of life than you ever imagined possible. *Let it happen to you!*

# ACKNOWLEDGMENTS

The stories of "happenings" which have been used are real life experiences and are taken from *Science of Mind* Magazine where they appeared, for the most part, under the general heading of "I Refused the Verdict."

The authors, original titles, and issues in which they appeared are as follows:

1. Miranda Snow Walton — "I Refused to Be a Cripple" — October 1958
2. Christopher West — "My Mental Muddle" — September 1958
3. W. R. Miller — " 'Problem' Solved!" — January 1958
4. Anna Stoddard — "I Found Freedom" — January 1956
5. Gus Goodman — "Health from an Old Trunk" — September 1956
6. Mary H. Boyles — "She Walked with God" — February 1957
7. Marjorie Alexander — "Release from Migraine" — February 1958
8. Catherine M. Cates — "You Don't Need Wings" — December 1957
9. Larry Barretto — "Chance in an Ordered World?" — February 1956
10. Thelma Olson — "You Set the Stage" — June 1957
11. Jane McLean — "I Fought Suicide, and Won!" — October 1956
12. Grace Ware — "I Do Not Accept the Delusion of Age" — November 1957
13. Annie S. Greenwood — "Business by the Carload" — December 1956
14. Elmer Grey — "The Course of Events" — August 1956
15. Maxine O'Brien — "I Was Forced to Better Myself" — November 1956
16. H. C. Hand — "Behind the Scenes of Life" — December 1958